For the Health of Your Marriage

~ *Living & Loving Life Together* ~

Mary A. Ford
Special Contributions
by Reverend James A. Ford, Jr.

Copyright © 2024 Mary A. Ford
www.duty2delightministries.com

Cover and interior design by Lisa Bell dba Radical Women
www.bylisabell.com

Publisher: Radical Women
PO Box 782
Granbury, TX 76048
817-269-9066

Print ISBN: 978-1-965561-03-4
eBook ISBN: 978-1-965561-04-1

DEDICATION

FOR THE HEALTH OF *Your Marriage* is dedicated to all couples who have committed to "doing marriage God's way"—according to the Word of God. May your marriage grow stronger, become energized, refreshed and more vibrant than ever before as you journey together through *"For the Health of Your Marriage."*

~Mary and James Ford, Jr.

"And if one prevails against him, two shall withstand him; and a threefold cord is not quickly broken."
Ecclesiastes: 4:12 (NKJV)

Contents

SPECIAL FEATURES

** A ***Focus Scripture*** is at the beginning of each devotion that relates to the marital topic of the day. Couples should meditate upon the scripture throughout the day and seek ways to put it into practice during the week.

** ***Action to Keep Attraction!*** This section is designed for couples to journal a list of "actions" each of them will take to put the things they learn into practice each day. What might start out as a "To-Do List" will quickly transform into a new way of "loving each other."

** ***A Prayer for Your Marriage*** is a special topical prayer by the authors designed to encourage couples to cultivate a healthy marriage according to God's plan.

** ***Prayer for His/ Her Heart*** is a section where husbands and wives journal their daily personal prayers specifically for their spouse and marriage.

INTRODUCTION

FOR THE HEALTH OF Your Marriage is a 21-day marriage devotional designed to encourage Christian couples to *ENJOY* the freedom and intimacy of Christ-centered marriage. Couples will experience how to tighten their marital ties as they study, pray, play, worship and apply biblical principles to their daily lives—each day growing closer in oneness, intimacy and embracing unconditional love!

Expect great things to happen in your marriage as you unwrap the joy of experiencing Jesus together as one. You will not only enjoy a fresh and rejuvenated marriage that will fulfill your needs and please and glorify God, but it will encourage others as they witness your marriage transformed into one that is *divinely designed by The Master!*

~ Mary A. Ford

"And the LORD God said, 'It is not good that man should be alone; I will make him a helper comparable to him.'"
Genesis 2:18-24 (NKJV)

"My Gift—Just Right for Me"
A Very Special Prayer of Devotion

LORD, YOU KNEW WHAT I would need even before I ever needed it. You knew what my heart would desire even before I ever had a desire for it. Before the earth's foundation was laid by your hands—Lord, you designed a very special *gift—Just Right for Me!*

You took the time to ensure that this special *gift* in human form had all the right ingredients—sincere humility, abundant love, profound compassion, and a quiet strength... just to name a few. But you also made sure to include a heart that was pure and an *Eros love* so deep for me all the world could see he indeed is—*Just Right for Me!*

Lord, you took your time when crafting this very special *gift*. But the time I spent waiting was well worth it because you made sure to include everything I would need—patience, knowledge, wisdom, tenderness and understanding—all these and so much more you poured generously into this special *gift* you made—*Just Right for Me!*

After you finished composing this one-of-a-kind masterpiece *gift* for me—you even took the time to make sure it was wrapped beautifully. To my surprise you made sure the wrapping was just the right color, texture, tone and size—then you topped it off with a big, beautiful bow of *unshakeable, unconditional LOVE!*

Then waiting until the right year, month, day, and hour in time... you presented me with my very special *gift*—a divinely designed man of God that could be my friend, my confidant, my lover, my husband, the priest of our home. *The one you kept just for me!*

Abba, you blessed me with a designer original! You sealed us with love eternal and unconditional! The *gift* of a *husband* that's one of a kind and made with only me in mind—and made to stand the test of time!

I thank you, LORD, for this very special *gift!* To you, LORD, all the praise I lift. Married life has been such a joy divine. So much peace I find—living with this *husband* of mine. You gave him to me just in time—because this special *gift* helps my little light shine. I just LOVE him, Lord—for I can see that he indeed is...*Just Right for Me!*

Eternally, Your Wife—Mary A. Ford

Day One

Blueprint for a Healthy Marriage

So, the Lord God caused a deep sleep to fall upon Adam; and while he slept, He took one of his ribs and closed up the flesh at that place. And the rib which the Lord God had taken from the man He made (fashioned, formed) into a woman, and He brought her and presented her to the man. Then Adam said, 'This is now bone of my bones, And flesh of my flesh; She shall be called Woman, because she was taken out of Man.' For this reason, a man shall leave his father and his mother and shall be joined to his wife; and they shall become one flesh. And the man and his wife were both naked and were not ashamed or embarrassed.

Genesis 2:21-24 (AMP)

MARRIAGE—The wedding day is what everyone prepares the most for, *BUT* it's *"The Marriage"* that needs the most preparation and maintenance. There are too many marriages out there on respirators...or that have totally flat lined! Too many marriages have taken one last breath before it all ends in divorce.

Divorce statistics from the CDC for 2019 indicate that every 42 seconds, there is one divorce in America. That equates to 86 divorces per hour, 2,046 divorces per day, 14,364 divorces per week, and 746,971 divorces per year. There are nearly 3 divorces in the time it takes for a couple to recite their wedding vows—approximately 2 minutes!

Were there tell-tell signs of retreating *health* of these marriages? Could something have been done to save these marriages? Well, perhaps or maybe not, but there certainly is something that can be done to save the marriages of those who are willing to try another way...*GOD's way!*

God's blueprint for a healthy marriage is outlined in his Word, beginning in *Genesis 2:21-24* for starts, then sprinkled throughout the bible. Let's take a look at some areas that will surely serve as a sound foundation to *build a healthy marriage:*

God's Three (3) Mandates for Marriage: Genesis 2:21-24

1. God designed marriage between man and woman.

2. God calls couples (man and woman) to live out their relationship for his glory.

3. God's design for marriage consists of a lifelong union between man and woman. God hates divorce! (Malachi 2:16)

Have a Godly Perspective on Marriage: Matthew 22:36-39

Love God and love your spouse—in that order! Build your marriage centered on Christ; specifically focused and centered on glorifying God through loving your spouse as Christ loves the church. Your marriage then becomes a testing ground for learning how to love like Jesus loves—unconditionally!

What God Joins Together, Let No Man Separate: Matthew 19:3-9

Being committed to honoring God through your marriage is a choice you make every day after saying *"I Do."* Divorce is a divine exception to human weaknesses. Instead of asking when is a divorce acceptable, ask *"When is remarriage acceptable in God's sight?"*

1. Unrepentant, immoral spouse. (Matthew 19:8-9)

2. Desertion of an unbelieving mate. (1 Corinthians 7:12-16)

FOR THE HEALTH OF YOUR MARRIAGE

3. Death of a spouse. (1 Corinthians 7:39)

4. Marital failure/divorce prior to conversion/salvation. (1 Corinthians 7:15)

Know How to Give and Receive Love: Romans 12:10

Learn to be kind and affectionate to one another; giving honor and preference to one another. Find ways to love your spouse the way they want to be loved. In other words, know what makes your spouse's *"boat float!"*

4-Essential Ingredients for a *"Healthy Marriage"*: Genesis 2:24-25

1. *Severance*—leave and cleave; break all ties (apron strings) with parents and cleave to your spouse. (Matthew 19:4-5)

2. *Permanence*—a lifelong union between man and woman. *"Joined together"* literally means to be bonded or glued together. Marriage is designed by God to be an impenetrable and everlasting relationship. (Matthew 19:6)

3. *Unity*—the two become one flesh. Unified oneness; but still uniquely you! (Matthew 19:6)

4. *Intimacy*—both were naked and not ashamed. Intimacy untarnished by sin! (Genesis 2:25)

Pride Can be Intoxicating, *but the Hangover is Hell!* Proverbs 16:18

Learning to appropriately apply these three little words can help save your marriage:

- *I am Sorry*

- *I forgive you*

- *I love you*

"Pride goes before destruction, and a haughty spirit before a fall."

Proverbs 16:18 (ESV)

Action to Keep Attraction

What actions will you and your spouse take to incorporate into your marriage the principles, practices, and lessons learned in this chapter? Write out your goals, plans, and strategies to achieve them on the lines below.

_____

_____

_____

_____

_____

_____

_____

_____

_____

_____

_____

_____

_____

_____

_____

_____

_____

_____

A Prayer for Your Marriage

Heavenly Father, I pray that this husband and wife will take the time to invest in the health of their marriage. Give them steadfast devotion as they embark upon this twenty-one-day journey. Allow them to truly see their mate's heart as they study, apply, pray and worship together. Bless them with a very special unconditional love that they may live out together each and every day in their marriage. Help them to see their spouse's love in their eyes whenever they look at them. Allow them to feel their spouses' love whenever they so gently hold each other's hand. Bless this couple to experience one another's love as they pray together daily. Give them a new revelation concerning their spouse—realizing that God designed their two hearts to beat together as one forever—two hearts pounding in the rhythm of one with so much passion they exuberant Eros and Agape love all rolled into one! Help them to recognize and embrace the truth that truly there is no one else they would rather take life's journey with—they are indeed better together!

Thank you, Abba, for hearing and answering this humble prayer for this couple seeking to do marriage your way, Yahweh! It's in Jesus' name I pray. Amen.

Have You Invested in The Health of Your Marriage TODAY?

Prayer for HIS/HER Heart

A Personal Prayer for Your Spouse and Marriage

Heavenly Father,

_____

_____

_____

_____

_____

_____

_____

_____

_____

_____

_____

_____

_____

_____

_____

_____

_____

Day Two

The Fallacy About Love

Love is patient, love is kind. It does not envy, it does not boast, it is not proud. It does not dishonor others, it is not self-seeking, it is not easily angered, it keeps no record of wrongs. Love does not delight in evil but rejoices with the truth. It always protects, always trusts, always hopes, and always perseveres. Love never fails.

1 Corinthians 13:4-8 (NIV)

SOME PEOPLE BELIEVE THAT it is impossible to love others like Christ loves us—unconditionally. Those who believe this are prone to place *"conditions"* upon their love for others—all based upon their own personal selfish feelings, desires and motives. But is this really *"true love"*? Well, if this were true love, then God would never have commanded believers to *"love your neighbor as yourself"* (Matthew 22:39b); nor would He have told husbands to *"love your wives, just as Christ also loved the church and gave Himself for her"* (Ephesians 5:25).

The biggest fallacy about love is that...*it's uncontrollable.* You may have heard (or even have said it yourself) that *"you can't help who you fall in love with"*. But is this true? If this were true, then why would God command us to do something that was utterly impossible or something that we could not control? That's because true love is not something that just happens or that you just fall into—but rather you make the freewill choice to love. You can choose to love regardless of the associated circumstances or conditions. Love is not based upon social or economic status, physical appearance, or even if all your desires are being met. Love is a CHOICE. And whether or not it endures is determined by your COMMITMENT to the one you choose to love.

Commitment—there's that word again! Have you ever really thought about what this word means in the realm of love and marriage? Many people entering marriage do so believing the fallacy that *"love is all we need"* to have a healthy, happy marriage. That fluttering butterfly feeling in the pit of your stomach when you see that special someone...or that smile that burst out on your face at the mere thought or mention of their name. Are these feelings of love enough to endure the test of time? Is *LOVE* really all you need? Is love really enough? Some of these emotions or feelings of love may soon pass after the honeymoon stage of marriage, but *true love*—love that's rooted and grounded in *commitment* will last forever! *Remember...*being committed to honoring God through your marriage is a CHOICE you make every single day after saying *"I Do"*.

The truth about true love is that it never fades or runs out. Love is so powerful and so important to God that He tells us in His Word that no matter who you are, what you have, what you do or what you have accomplished—if you don't have LOVE, then you have nothing, and your living is not really living at all! When all else fades away, true love is the only thing that will stand the test of time (I Corinthians 13:1-8).

Jesus taught that loving God first and then loving others as you do yourself are both equally necessary for all believers—this is unconditional love in action (Matthew 22:36-40). True love begins with the act of giving—not receiving. You worship God when you love and sacrifice for your spouse. God's Word says to *"Love one another with brotherly affection. Outdo one another in showing honor"* (Romans 12:10). When this scripture is applied to your marriage, you will no longer require your spouse to *"make you happy,"* but rather you will seek to find ways to honor your commitment to God through your marriage.

St. Francis said, *"Seek to understand before seeking to be understood."* This is a seed of selflessness that will yield a bumper crop of unconditional love towards your spouse. The key to *"true love"* is *unselfishness*—a sign of unconditional love in action demonstrated first by Christ.

Remember... "Commitment adds muscle to your marriage when love becomes weakened."
Invest in the Health of Your Marriage...TODAY!

Action to Keep Attraction

What actions will you and your spouse take to incorporate into your marriage the principles, practices, and lessons learned from this chapter? Write out your goals, plans, and strategies to achieve them on the lines below.

_____

_____

_____

_____

_____

_____

_____

_____

_____

_____

_____

_____

_____

_____

A Prayer for Your Marriage

Heavenly Father, teach this couple to love like Christ—unconditionally. Help them to see the good in each other and to love their spouse even when they are unlovely. Give this husband and wife a heart of compassion and eyes that can see past their pain to a soul crying out for genuine love!

Lord GOD, your love is perfect—allow the spirit of your love to permeate the atmosphere in this couple's home and captivate each of their hearts so that they might live out the evidence of love as captured in 1 Corinthians 13:4-8. Teach this couple to have the kind of Eros and Agape love that can come only from their wills being totally surrendered to yours. It's in Jesus' name I pray. Amen.

Have You Invested in The Health of Your Marriage TODAY?

Prayer for HIS/HER Heart

A Personal Prayer for Your Spouse and Marriage

Heavenly Father,

_____

_____

_____

_____

_____

_____

_____

_____

_____

_____

_____

_____

_____

_____

_____

_____

_____

_____

_____

Day Three

The Ties That Bind

> *And the Lord God said, it is not good that man should be alone: I will make him a help meet for him. Therefore, shall a man leave his father and his mother, and shall cleave unto his wife: and they shall be one flesh.*
>
> Genesis 2:18, 24 (NKJV)

EVERYONE WANTS TO KNOW the "secret to a perfect marriage". Well, the truth be told, there is NO perfect marriage...because there are NO perfect people. Marriage allows God to take two imperfect, broken people and put them back together as ONE...with CHRIST being the glue that bonds eternally. Husband—Wife—Christ. That's three-cord harmony!

There is no book on marriage that you can buy that will provide better guidance, direction and instruction on building a healthy marriage than the bible. The formula for a successful marriage is built upon the biblical truths of God. A biblical marriage is centered on Christ and is specifically dedicated to glorifying God. The bible describes *the church* (Christians) as the *spiritual bride of Christ*. So, since we are the church (the bride of Christ), then that would make Jesus Christ our spiritual spouse. Therefore, we can remain *committed* to each other as husband and wife as long as we remain *committed* to Christ; and that means *doing marriage* His way (Ephesians 5:22-33).

Our *spiritual love relationship* with God is vital, but He never intended it to stop there! God's plan from the beginning of time was for man to have someone to show *physical love* to in a *spiritual way*. I'm talking about an unconditional, sacrificial, super-natural kind of love! God intended for us to *enjoy His love through our spouse*. This kind of love relationship between a husband and wife can only exist through Christ. His love frees us up to love our spouse as Christ loves the church...and our spouse will be free to love us right back! *"The Lord God said, 'It is not good for the man to be alone. I will make a helper suitable for him.'"* (Genesis 2:18 NIV).

You are probably asking yourself, *"Well, what went wrong with marriage?"*

"What makes it so hard to love like Christ?"

And last, but not least, *"Why does it seem almost impossible to stay out of divorce court?"*

The short and most accurate response to each of these questions is...*SIN*. Yes, *sin* is the cause of the breakdown in the *"permanence"* of marriage. Instead of trusting God to heal and restore broken marriages through obedience to His word, it's much easier to chalk it up to *"irreconcilable differences"* and head to divorce court. *Sin* has caused today's culture to give a *"green light"* to *"redefining marriage"* where society no longer abides by God's definition of marriage *between one man and one woman*. *Sin* is the cause of many leaving the *"sanctity of marriage"* and embracing with open arms the satanic concept of *"try it before you buy it"* (shacking) and *"what they don't know won't hurt"* (infidelity) mentality. And the *selfishness of sin* is the reason why many have forsaken seeking to love *unselfishly* and *unconditionally* like Christ. *"Jesus replied, 'Love the Lord your God with all your heart and with all your soul and with all your mind.' This is the first and greatest commandment. And the second is like it: 'Love your neighbor as yourself"* (Matthew 22: 37, 39).

That's what went wrong with marriage, but the real question is *"how can we do it right?"* Well, here's a few tips on how to **SUCCEED** in having a *Healthy Marriage:*

- **Start** thinking *"positive thoughts"* about your marriage. No more STINKING THINKING!

- **Understand** *"who"* is really in control of your marriage—GOD! Three cords are not easily broken!

- **Concentrate** on *"building UP"* your marriage—NOT tearing it down!

- **Care** about the *"Health"* of your marriage. Do regular checkups with your spouse!

- **Exceed** what your *"spouse expects"* of you. Don't settle for mediocre or just enough to pacify—remember, your gold is to GLORIFY!

- **Expand** your *"love tactics"* to meet your spouse's needs—Think outside the box and maybe even outside of your comfort zone!

- **Dedicate** your marriage as a *"representative"* of God's love for the church, as a godly example for others and to be used for God's purposes.

"And if one prevails against him, two shall withstand him; and a threefold cord is not quickly broken."

Ecclesiastes: 4:12 (KJV)

Action to Keep Attraction

What actions will you and your spouse take to incorporate into your marriage the principles, practices, and lessons learned from this chapter? Write out your goals, plans, and strategies to achieve them on the lines below.

_____

_____

_____

_____

_____

_____

_____

_____

_____

_____

_____

_____

_____

_____

A Prayer for Your Marriage

Heavenly Father, Bless this husband and wife with forgiving hearts and a desire to do marriage your way and not their own. Raise up this Christian marriage as a shining example for those that may be struggling.

Help the husband to love the Lord with his whole heart and love his wife like Christ loves the church. Bless and enable the husband to be the provider, head of household, divine leader, and loving and affectionate priest of his own home. I pray that the wife will support, encourage, and respect her own husband as unto the Lord with joy—trusting the God in her husband to lead as Christ would lead.

Help this couple to submit to one another, commit to praying together and to consistently study God's word together in order to cultivate an atmosphere of love, respect and peace in their home. Allow oneness, unity, commitment, unconditional love and sanctity to rule and reign over and within the bedroom of this Christian marriage.

Most of all, let selflessness and forgiveness be abundant, allowing the husband and wife to show humility of spirit as they submit to Christ and experience three cord harmony that is not easily broken!

Father God, help this couple to show physical love to one another in a spiritual way—an unconditional, sacrificial, super-natural kind of love—just as you intended! It's in the name of Jesus I humbly pray...Amen!

Have You Invested in The Health of Your Marriage TODAY?

Prayer for HIS/HER Heart

A Personal Prayer for Your Spouse and Marriage

Heavenly Father,

_____

_____

_____

_____

_____

_____

_____

_____

_____

_____

_____

_____

_____

_____

_____

_____

_____

_____

Day Four

What Women Want

My beloved is exquisitely handsome and ruddy, outstanding among ten thousand. His head is like [precious] gold, pure gold; His hair is [curly] like clusters of dates and black as a raven. His eyes are like doves beside streams of water, bathed in milk and reposed in their setting. His cheeks are like a bed of balsam, banks of sweet, fragrant herbs. His lips are lilies dripping sweet-scented myrrh. His hands are rods of gold set with beryl; His abdomen is a figure of carved ivory inlaid with sapphires. His legs are [strong and steady] pillars of alabaster set upon pedestals of fine gold. His appearance is like Lebanon, stately and choice as the cedars. His mouth is full of sweetness; Yes, he is altogether lovely and desirable. This is my beloved, and this is my friend.

Song of Solomon 5:10-16 (AMP)

MANY BELIEVE THE SONG of Solomon to be a collection of songs, but rather it should be viewed as a type of drama or lyric poem celebrating a relationship between a man and woman that exuberates a healthy, growing love that leads to maturity in marriage. Intimacy and oneness in marriage is not just about *"getting physical,"* but more about the journey to that destination!

There are many women who desire to be married, and some women who are married that desire to be single! But how many women ask *"What does God want for me"* before they say, *"I do"*? Does God want you to have a husband? Does God's promises even include you having a spouse? The Bible says *"yes."* God's original plan was for man and woman to become one in marriage. Genesis 2:18 says, *"And the Lord God said, 'It is not good that man should be alone; I will make him a helper comparable to him'"*. So, if God's plan for man and woman is marriage...and your desire is also to be married...then talk to God about your mate and how you can be more intentional in meeting their needs.

After all, God never intended for your *spiritual love relationship* with him to stop there. God's plan from the beginning of time was for man to have someone to show *physical love* to in a *spiritual way*. So, ask yourself *"Do I really know/understand what my husband's needs are in marriage?"* And better yet, *"Do I even know/understand what my own needs are in marriage?"* Many times, spouses don't meet each other's needs due to ignorance, not selfishness or unwillingness. If this is the case, then to what extent are you willing to go to become better at meeting your spouse's needs?

Any of us can fall victim to an extra-marital affair if our basic needs as a spouse are not met. Many polls and surveys have been done, but the following five (5) basic needs are most often shared by wives:

- *Affection*
- *Conversation*
- *Openness/Honesty*
- *Financial Support*
- *Family Commitment*

A friendship turned *affair* is usually not based on physical attraction, but rather on emotional attraction—someone's needs being met outside of the marriage. When needs go unmet in a marriage, they are oftentimes replaced with frustration in place of love, which is detrimental to nurturing intimacy and oneness in marriage. God has this to say about meeting our mate's needs: "*Let the husband render to his wife the affection due her, and likewise also the wife to her husband. The wife does not have authority over her own body, but the husband does. And likewise, the husband does not have authority over his own body, but the wife does. Do not deprive one another except with consent for a time that you may give yourselves to fasting and prayer; and come together again so that Satan does not tempt you because of your lack of self-control*" (1 Corinthians 7:3-5).

Spend some time reflecting on the list of *five basic needs of a woman* in marriage previously shared in this chapter. Are any of these needs not being met in your marriage? Are there any other needs not being met in your marriage? How does it make you feel to have the EXCLUSIVE right to meet your mate's intimate needs and vice versa? Now ask yourself what might you have to *give up* or *change* to meet your spouse's needs?

In the next chapter, you will discover the *five (5) basic needs of the husband*. I encourage and challenge you to become aware of each other's needs...and then *learn* how to meet them! After all, the goal in marriage is not just friendship—*it's ONENESS!*

> "*May he kiss me with the kisses of his mouth*"! *[Solomon arrives, she turns to him, saying,]. For your love is better than wine. The aroma of your oils is fragrant and pleasing; your name is perfume poured out; therefore the maidens love you.*"
> Song of Solomon 1:2-3 (AMP)

Remember... "It's NOT about comfort, it's all about LOVE!"

Action to Keep Attraction

What actions will you and your spouse take to incorporate into your marriage the principles, practices, and lessons learned in this chapter? Write out your goals, plans, and strategies to achieve them on the lines below.

Be sure to incorporate your answers to the questions posed in this chapter.

_____

_____

_____

_____

_____

_____

_____

_____

_____

_____

_____

_____

_____

A Prayer for Your Marriage

Heavenly Father, I come praying for the healing and restoration of hurt, broken and failed marriages, and for the reuniting of families as a whole unit.

Holy Spirit speak to the hearts of husbands and wives, flooding them with the overwhelming desire to meet each other's needs and reclaim the passion, fire, and desire for each other that will demonstrate in physical form Christ's love for the Church.

Penetrate hearts with selflessness, forgiveness, and unconditional love for one another and give them humble spirits so that their lifestyles will line up with Your WORD and their prayers may be heard!

LORD, no matter how dead the marriage situation may look, increase their believing faith in your ability to intervene supernaturally and do the impossible! YOU, ELOHIM, can breathe into a dead marriage new life, restore that which the locusts have eaten, and resurrect any dead thing!

Jehovah Tsaba—The Lord Our Warrior—rise up and wage war against the enemy on behalf of Christian marriages! It's in Jesus' mighty, matchless, and miraculous name I pray...Amen!

Have You Invested in The Health of Your Marriage TODAY?

Prayer for HIS/HER Heart

A Personal Prayer for Your Spouse and Marriage

Heavenly Father,

_____

_____

_____

_____

_____

_____

_____

_____

_____

_____

_____

_____

_____

_____

_____

_____

_____

_____

Day Five

What Men Want

By Rev. James A. Ford, Jr.

An excellent wife, who can find? For her worth is far above jewels.

Proverbs 31:10 (NAS95)

WHEN ONE ASKS MEN what they want, you will get many different answers. Some men will say a better job so they can make more money. Others will say a nice home and car...and the list goes on and on. When it comes to marriage and what men want, there have been many books written about this subject. However, based upon my experience in counseling married couples over the years, I have found that most men would agree that the following five things are not only *"wants"*, but are much needed to have a fulfilling marriage:

1. Unconditional Love and Acceptance

2. Sexual Intimacy

3. Companionship

4. Encouragement

5. Affirmation

You see, when it comes to a *wife,* men often look for more specific *needs.* For example, is she pretty to look at? Her shape and size. Is she successful and prosperous? Does she have kids, and if so, how many? Are there financial debts and issues that could affect the relationship? I found in my years of doing pre-marital counseling that often times the things men think least about is what is most important—*Does she have a relationship with God?*

The Bible says, *"He who finds a wife finds a good thing, and obtains favor from the Lord"* Proverbs 18:22. However, spiritual intimacy with the Lord has not been a high priority on most men's list when looking for a wife, until perhaps after the wedding. So I suggest that men *pray* and ask God's guidance when trying to *"find a good thang".*

I remember before I got married how I sought the Lord in prayer. Being a divorcee, I didn't want to make another mistake, so I prayed and asked the Lord to lead me to the right mate suitable for me. *"Therefore, I say to you, all things for which you pray and ask, believe that you have received them, and they will be granted you"* Mark 11:24. When I prayed this scripture, it came to pass. You see, it's easy to accept better, but we must be willing to wait for *God's best!*

When I was looking for *my wife,* I wanted the kind of wife God had for me. So I prayed and looked at women how God looked at them—*from the inside out.* It's very important to find a wife who loves God first and will love you as a man of God. I like to say, *"If you can't see her heart, then let her go!"* Don't settle—trust God. When you trust God with finding a spouse, then things will go better in the marriage as you both allow the Lord to be the third cord that binds you together.

Here is something my father and grandfather taught me at an early age that could help save your marriage. They said, *"Son, when you are blessed to find the right kind of wife God wants for you, remember to use these words often, 'please forgive me' and 'I'm sorry, you were right.'"* I can honestly tell you that these few words, when applied at the right times, have kept me out of a lot of trouble with my wife! Great advice and sound wisdom, so I pass it on to the husbands reading this now—don't delay, start putting it into practice today!

There is a reason we men should not just look at outward beauty when searching for a wife. In Proverbs 31:30 it says, *"Charm is deceitful, and beauty is vain, but a woman who fears the Lord, she shall be praised."* There is more to a woman than skin deep. One needs to talk and find out truly how much she loves the Lord. Her spiritual intimacy with the Lord is important if you want a wife who will grow with you in the Lord. If you can't read the Word or pray with her then you may be in trouble. Look for the red signs and don't ignore them because of what you see on the outside. They can help keep you out of trouble!

Remember, God knows what you need better than you do, so trust Him. Pray for direction on who to date and what kind of godly wife you should be looking for to be your lifelong partner. She might be right in front of you, but you need God to open your spiritual eyes to see her. God will always give you what you need, not just what you want! Pray—Seek—Find—and Trust God for the results.

> *"She does him good and not evil all the days of her life."*
> Proverbs 31:12

~THINK ABOUT IT~

If you have been searching for the right woman to be in your life with no luck, then try God's way. Read what *He says* about the kind of wife *He wants* you to have. Pray for guidance as you seek for her in life. Pray for God to prepare her for you and you for her. Be honest and real with each other when you find her. Openly and honestly express what each of you is looking for in the relationship as a lifelong mate. Look to see her how God sees her. Trust God to show you her spiritually.

Action to Keep Attraction

Meditate on Proverbs 31: 10-12. Write out on the lines below your personal prayer for a godly wife. Ask God to show you how to be properly prepared for her and to know she is the one for you. If already married, then write out your goals, plans, and strategies to incorporate things learned from this chapter on the lines below.

_____

_____

_____

_____

_____

_____

_____

_____

_____

_____

_____

_____

A Prayer for Your Marriage

Father God, help my fellow brothers to seek you as they look for a wife. Lead them to be the godly man you want them to be for that woman. Help the man praying this prayer to serve you, Father, with all his heart. As he looks for the woman of his dreams help them to see her through the lens of spiritual insight. To see with spiritual vision that she truly loves you first with all her heart. By this he will know that she will love him also.

Lord, help godly men everywhere to always seek you for his spouse and trust you for the outcome! It's in the mighty name of Jesus I pray. Amen.

"Behold, how beautiful you are, my darling, Behold, how beautiful you are! Your eyes are dove's eyes. You have ravished my heart and given me courage, my sister, my bride; you have ravished my heart and given me courage with a single glance of your eyes, with one jewel of your necklace. How beautiful is your love, my sister, my [promised] bride! How much better is your love than wine, and the fragrance of your oils than all kinds of balsam and spices. Your lips, my bride, drip honey [as the honeycomb]; Honey and milk are under your tongue, and the fragrance of your garments is like the fragrance of Lebanon."
Song of Solomon 1:15, 4:9-11 (AMP)

Have You Invested in The Health of Your Marriage TODAY?

Prayer for HIS/HER Heart

A Personal Prayer for Your Spouse and Marriage

Heavenly Father,

_____

_____

_____

_____

_____

_____

_____

_____

_____

_____

_____

_____

_____

_____

_____

_____

Day Six

How Deep Is Your Love?

There is no fear in love [dread does not exist]. But perfect (complete, full-grown) love drives out fear, because fear involves [the expectation of divine] punishment, so the one who is afraid [of God's judgment] is not perfected in love [has not grown into a sufficient understanding of God's love].

I John 4:18 (AMP)

A SONGWRITER ONCE ASKED, *"What's love got to do with it?"* Well, God's Word tells us that *LOVE* has everything to do with it! There are many marriages simply surviving and not thriving because husbands and wives are *afraid* to truly *love one another unconditionally*. Unconditional love and commitment are two essential ingredients needed to form a lasting marriage that will bring joy and happiness to the couple and bring glory and honor to God.

Living with insecurities and fear of being hurt, or not having your love reciprocated, can ruin marital relationships because it prevents intimacy and oneness. Deep within, you long to be closer to your spouse, but are afraid to let the real you shine through. You sincerely desire intimacy and oneness, but the thought of opening up to that vulnerability scares you into unresponsiveness. Taking the limits off and removing the boundaries that may have functioned as a safety net in the past can be really scary, but when you open up your heart to unconditional love, your marriage will come alive in ways you've never experienced before!

God's Word says *"perfect love (complete, full-grown love) drives out fear."* This means real love (God's love) uproots and casts out fear. Insecurities vanish and love takes its place, rising into full and complete intimacy and oneness in your marriage!

Ask yourself this question, *"How deep is my Love for my spouse?"* Well, the best measuring stick is God's Word. Below is what the Bible says your love should look like toward others, including your spouse *(I Corinthians 13:4-8).*

- Love is *patient*

- Love is *kind*

- Love is *not jealous*

- Love *does not brag*

- Love is *not proud*

- Love is *not rude*

- Love is *not selfish*

- Love *cannot be made angry easily*

- Love *does not remember wrongs* done against it or *hold grudges*

- Love is *never happy when others do wrong,* but it is always *happy with the truth.*

- Love *never gives up* on people—it *never stops trusting, never loses hope,* and *never quits.*

- Love *never fails!*

Well, how did you do when measuring your love for your spouse against God's Word? When we realize just how much God truly loves us, then that frees us up to love others. We no longer have to put on a false demeanor or be concerned about what others think, because we are secure in Jesus' love. Love takes the focus off you and puts the focus on your spouse—that's love unlimited!

"Why not let Jesus' love bubble over on your spouse today?"

Action to Keep Attraction

What actions will you and your spouse take to incorporate into your marriage the principles, practices, and lessons learned in this chapter? Write out your goals, plans, and strategies to achieve them on the lines below.

_____

_____

_____

_____

_____

_____

_____

_____

_____

_____

_____

_____

_____

_____

_____

A Prayer for Your Marriage

Heavenly Father, I pray that this couple will allow your love to bubble up and over into their marriage each and every day. Allow them to see your love every time they look into each other's eyes. Allow them to feel your love every time they kiss. Endow them with your love in every warm embrace. Allow them to express their love in new and refreshing ways!

Father, show them how to protect each other's heart. Always allow their love for each other to never run cold or lukewarm, but to remain HOT—Holy, Oneness, Thankful! I pray that this marriage will be centered in Christ, rooted in unconditional LOVE one for another, and sealed for life through the power of The Holy Spirit.

It's in the strong and mighty Name of Jesus Christ I pray...Amen!

Have You Invested in The Health of Your Marriage TODAY?

Prayer for HIS/HER Heart

A Personal Prayer for Your Spouse and Marriage

Heavenly Father,

_____

_____

_____

_____

_____

_____

_____

_____

_____

_____

_____

_____

_____

_____

_____

Day Seven

With This Ring... I Thee Wed

Awake, O north wind, and come, O south wind! Blow upon my garden, let its spices flow. Let my beloved come to his garden and eat its choicest fruits.

Song of Solomon 4:16 (ESV)

MANY DIVORCES ARE A result of some type of romanticized expectation of one or both spouses that fades away with time. Change takes place—weight gain, age lines, hair loss... and the list goes on and on! Then you wonder why your spouse doesn't *"make me happy anymore"* and *"where did our marriage go wrong?"*

Truth be told, no one can truly make you happy or unhappy. This is a personal choice—regardless of your situation or the circumstances—you choose your state of being. Therefore, don't believe the devil's lies—expose and expel that which inhibits happiness in your marriage and embrace the unimaginable—nothing's too hard for God!

Although, it can sometimes be challenging to "keep the fire burning" after the honeymoon stage of marriage wears off. So I recommend a daily dose of the *Song of Solomon* to keep the home fire burning. If you have not read the book of *Song of Solomon* to your spouse, then you have missed out on the greatest aphrodisiac of them all! It's never too late, so start reading today.

I praise God that my husband and I share a very special love we live out together every day in our marriage. Not because we are perfect. It's because we choose to love each other unconditionally. I *see* my husband's love for me in his eyes when he looks at me and when he smiles at me so sweetly. I *feel* my husband's love for me when he hugs me and holds my hand so gently. I *experience* my husband's love for me as he prays over me daily and shares God's Word with me so freely. There is no one else I'd rather *"do life"* with—my lover, my friend, my confidant, my husband. Two hearts beating together as one forever; pounding with so much passion that Eros and Agape love is exuberated... all rolled into one. *We are indeed better together!*

The Challenge—Forever I Do!

(Recipe for a Happy Marriage)

God's design for marriage includes *"forever after,"* so I challenge each of you to seriously commit to putting the following *Recipe for a Happy Marriage* into practice every day for the remainder of this devotional.

1. ***PRAY*** for your spouse and marriage daily.

2. ***WATER*** yourself and your spouse with GOD's Word.

3. Develop a ***PRAISE*** and ***WORSHIP*** lifestyle together.

4. ***SPEAK LIFE*** into your marriage daily.

5. ***ANTICIPATE*** God's ***FAVOR*** over your marriage.

6. ***ENCOURAGE*** your spouse ***DAILY.***

7. ***LOVE*** your spouse ***TODAY*** like tomorrow is not promised.

When wholeheartedly followed, you will notice your marriage becoming sweeter and sweeter as this challenge becomes a *CHOICE* in your daily journey to—***Forever I Do!***

Don't forget to share this recipe with other couples—Bon appétit!

Action to Keep Attraction

What actions will you and your spouse take to incorporate into your marriage the principles, practices, and lessons learned in this chapter? Write out your goals, plans, and strategies to achieve them on the lines below.

_____

_____

_____

_____

_____

_____

_____

_____

_____

_____

_____

_____

_____

A Prayer for Your Marriage

Heavenly Father, pour out your spirit of unconditional love on this marriage today. Turn the heart of the husband toward the wife and turn the wife's heart toward her husband. Bind this marriage together with the third cord of Christ that is not easily broken. Allow peace to be their pillow at night and joy to surround them with the morning light! Fortify their faith and help them face each day TOGETHER so nothing will shake their love, commitment, and unity.

These blessings I pray upon this husband and wife as they seek to honor Christ in their marriage. Let your perfect will be done—it's in the name of Jesus I pray and praise always. Amen.

Have You Invested in The Health of Your Marriage TODAY?

Prayer for HIS/HER Heart

A Personal Prayer for Your Spouse and Marriage

Heavenly Father,

_____

_____

_____

_____

_____

_____

_____

_____

_____

_____

_____

_____

_____

_____

49

Day Eight

Can we Talk?

You are jealous and covet [what others have] and your lust goes unfulfilled; so, you murder. You are envious and cannot obtain [the object of your envy]; so, you fight and battle. You do not have because you do not ask [it of God]. You ask [God for something] and do not receive it, because you ask with wrong motives [out of selfishness or with an unrighteous agenda], so that [when you get what you want] you may spend it on your [hedonistic] desires.

James 4:2-3 (AMP)

IN A WORLD WHERE abnormal is presented as "the norm," it makes it difficult at best for most to truly know what a *"healthy relationship"* actually looks and feels like. In today's society, we are presented with the pictures of relationships filled with toxicity, drama, and mistrust. When presented with a blueprint (the Bible) for establishing and maintaining a healthy marital relationship that is calm, kind, caring, drama-free, and non-toxic and doesn't require making painful sacrifices, you wonder if this could truly be achievable. According to the Bible, the answer is—*yes.*

Effective communication is a vital key to a healthy marriage. Slowly reread James 4:2-3 and meditate on how it might apply to your marriage. Many times, the biggest conflicts in marriage can happen over the smallest of things... all because of *a failure to communicate!* This type of conflict can easily pull couples apart instead of motivating oneness.

Therefore, make the commitment to "pull together" instead of allowing poor communication and marital conflicts pull you apart. Below are a few helpful nuggets that will help to *"talk things out"* instead of *"battling it out."*

1. Make special efforts to engage in *quality conversations* with your spouse.

2. Know what *type of conversationalist* you and your spouse are: 1) flowing fountain, 2) babbling brook, 3) muddy waters, 4) Dead Sea, or 5) a refreshing stream. This might require you to *listen more than you talk!*

3. Before you talk to your spouse about a problem, *talk to God first—PRAY about it!*

4. Don't expect your spouse to meet needs that *ONLY GOD can meet in your life.* Ask God to meet all needs in His sovereignty.

5. Nobody wins the *"blame game"* in marriage. Don't focus on what you believe your spouse did wrong, but rather ask God to *"show me, myself"* in this conflict, then own up to it if you are wrong. If you are right, don't make it a hammer to beat some sense into your spouse. (Matthew 7:3-5)

6. *Don't ignore the conflict* between you and your spouse. Ignoring the problem will not make it go away, but it will actually get worse if left unattended. (Philippians 2:3-4; Ephesians 4:26)

7. *Don't seek to be understood before you seek to understand where your spouse is coming from.* This is difficult because it goes against human nature. Everyone wants to be heard and understood, so you must be very intentional to shift the focus from *what you want to what your spouse needs.* Trust GOD to help you.

8. Understand the difference between reconciliation and resolution. *Reconciliation means to reestablish the relationship* and resolution

means to resolve an issue through total agreement. Good luck with that happening. *Sometimes you must agree to* disagree but always focus on allowing reconciliation to blossom in your marriage.

The old adage *"talk is cheap"* doesn't apply here, because a good heart-to-heart conversation with your spouse, while applying the above tips, can be worth more than gold and silver.

Just remember these three little words when it comes to addressing conflict and fostering a healthy marital relationship... "Can we talk"?

Action to Keep Attraction

What actions will you and your spouse take to incorporate into your marriage the principles, practices, and lessons learned in this chapter? Write out your goals, plans, and strategies to achieve them on the lines below.

_____

_____

_____

_____

_____

_____

_____

_____

_____

_____

_____

_____

_____

_____

A Prayer for Your Marriage

Heavenly Father, I pray that this couple will humble themselves in your presence; asking you to enter their marital conflicts before they ask others their opinions. Help them to check egos at the alter and trust your divine power to heal every hurt, right every wrong, make the crocked straight and the rough places smooth.

Jesus, do what only you can do as this couple puts their trust in you. It's in your mighty name I pray. Amen.

Have You Invested in The Health of Your Marriage TODAY?

Prayer for HIS/HER Heart

A Personal Prayer for Your Spouse and Marriage

Heavenly Father,

_____

_____

_____

_____

_____

_____

_____

_____

_____

_____

_____

_____

_____

Day Nine

Choose Your Weapon!

May the God who gives endurance and encouragement give you the same attitude of mind toward each other that Christ Jesus had, so that with one mind and one voice you may glorify the God and Father of our Lord Jesus Christ. Accept one another, then, just as Christ accepted you, in order to bring praise to God.
Romans 15:5-7 (NIV)

IT'S NOT EASY TO talk about healthy marriages when yours may be on a respirator! On the other hand, your marriage may be going well. But what happens when things are headed down the wrong street? Perhaps your marriage is not hot or cold, but sort of lukewarm—you both would rather avoid each other than to actually sit down and have a good old heart-to-heart conversation. In fact, it may seem the only time you see sparks and fire in your relationship is when you are arguing.

Oftentimes, couples quarrel because of differences in opinions or when they don't see things the same way about certain areas of their lives, such as finances, raising children or spending quality time together, etc. The old adage "opposites attract" is true to a certain degree. Sometimes, the very things that are different about your spouse is what actually attracted you to them the most. This is not unusual, because God made us all different so we can complement and complete each other. Where one may be lacking, the other may be stronger. This was by God's divine design, so why not consult the creator when seeking direction and advice on how to handle these *"differences"* when they are no longer a delight and cause conflict in your marriage?

Below are a few biblical lessons on how to *"fight fair"* and turn *conflict* into *revelation* that will strengthen your marriage.

- **Embrace your differences so you can learn and grow in your relationship**—accept the fact that God made men and women not only different physically, but in the way we think, act, respond, work, shop, and the list goes on and on. So, don't expect your spouse to *"think"* like you do or *"respond"* like you do in certain situations (Genesis 1:27). Remember, because of those differences you each bring a special outlook to the situation that would not be present otherwise. The Bible says to *"Accept one another, then, just as Christ accepted you, in order to bring praise to God."* In other words, you complete each other (Romans 15:7).

- **Let's Agree to Disagree**—this means setting aside your own hurt, anger, and bitterness and pursuing peace in the relationship overall (Romans 12:18).

- **Defeating Selfishness**—it's okay not to prove you are right all the time! Practice looking out for your spouse's personal interest more than you do your own (Philippians 2:3-8).

- **Don't trade insult for insult**—try returning an insult with a sincere blessing to turn things around (1 Peter 3:8-9).

- **Loving Confrontation**—confronting your spouse with grace and tactfulness can mean the difference between having a "happy home" and "living on a battlefield." To confront your spouse *lovingly* requires wisdom, patience, and humility (Philippians 2:1-2).

- **Practice Patience with each other**—making allowance for each other's faults because of your love. This is not easy, but practice makes perfect. (Ephesians 4:2).

- **Be willing to forgive and be forgiven**—cast away resentment and a desire to punish your spouse—none of us are perfect. (Matthew 6:14-15).

*Remember... When you feel angry, resentful, or disappointed with your spouse, then is the perfect time to go to God in prayer—**CHOOSE THE RIGHT WEAPON!***

Action to Keep Attraction

What actions will you and your spouse take to incorporate into your marriage the principles, practices, and lessons learned in this chapter? Write out your goals, plans, and strategies to achieve them on the lines below.

_____

_____

_____

_____

_____

_____

_____

_____

_____

_____

_____

_____

_____

_____

_____

_____

_____

A Prayer for Your Marriage

Heavenly Father, I pray that you set this couple's desires on fire for each other and give them a passion to please one another. Replace selfishness with selflessness. Uproot unforgiveness and plant compassion. Turn hearts of stone into hearts of flesh that will yield unconditional love. Open their spiritual eyes to see one another through the eyes of Christ—always relying on PRAYER as the best weapon to overcome conflict and receive divine instruction and intervention. Stir up a love so deep and fulfilling within them that it will overcome any obstacles that may arise—allowing this marriage to be a beacon of light, giving testimony of God's goodness, mercy, and grace!

It's in the mighty name of Jesus I pray. Amen.

Have You Invested in The Health of Your Marriage TODAY?

Prayer for HIS/HER Heart

A Personal Prayer for Your Spouse and Marriage

Heavenly Father,

Day Ten

The Heart of the Matter

> *They said, "Moses permitted a man to write a certificate of*
> *divorce and send her away."*
> *"It was because your hearts were hard that Moses wrote you this*
> *law," Jesus replied.*
>
> Mark 10:4-5 (NIV)

IN MARK 10, JESUS began to teach his followers, as was his custom, and a group of unbelievers (Pharisees) rose from the crowd to test him with questions regarding marriage and divorce. They asked, *"Is it lawful for a man to divorce his wife?"*

Jesus, being well aware of their motive behind their question, simply replied, *"What did Moses command you?"*

Of course, these scholarly men responded with the correct answer according to the Mosaic law, but Jesus knew their question and response was not coming from a place of *love*, so he pointed them back to the root of the matter—an unforgiving heart.

*"'It was because your hearts were hard that Moses wrote you this law,' Jesus replied." (*Mark 10:5 NIV).

To forgive or not to forgive—*is that the question?* Jesus made it crystal clear that God's plan from the beginning of creation for husband and wife was never divorce, but rather for them to live out their lives together, becoming as one flesh (vs. 6-9). When we learn to truly practice the *power of forgiveness*, many of the *"irreconcilable differences"* will dissolve and be replaced with unconditional love.

However, the power of forgiveness is often underestimated and mistaken for weakness. But in reality, it's just the opposite. It takes strength of the will to go against every fleshly desire to *"hold a grudge"* or to *"make them suffer"* by withholding forgiveness. On the other hand, unforgiveness is a road leading to hurt, pain, and a *callused heart*. It can only result in a fatal outcome for all involved.

So, how do we forgive when it still hurts so badly? By praying and asking God *"to give you a new heart and put a new spirit within you"* and to *"take the heart of stone out of your flesh and give you a heart of flesh."* (Ezekiel 36:26). Then, compassion can replace unforgiveness and allow you to reflect a Christlike heart toward your spouse, which leads to healing and restoration of your marriage.

This change in the condition of your *heart* will help cultivate an atmosphere in your home for unconditional love to grow. 1 Corinthians, Chapter 13 is known as *"The Love Chapter."* This is mainly because it teaches us about the *"more excellent gift"* of *LOVE!* It shows us what true, God-centered love looks like in action when applied, not only as individual believers, but to our marriages as well. *"Love is patient, love is kind. It does not envy, it does not boas, it is not proud. It does not dishonor others, it is not self-seeking, it is not easily angered, and it keeps no record of wrongs Love does not delight in evil but rejoices with the truth. It always protects, always trusts, always hopes, always perseveres. Love never fails."* (1 Corinthians 13: 4-8).

~THINK ABOUT IT~

Showing love (Christlike love) is NOT conditional, but it is unconditional in nature—not dependent on what your spouse does or does not do. Read and meditate on the following questions and then write out your *plan of action* to apply what you have learned in the next section.

- Which do you exhibit most in your marriage—forgiveness or unforgiveness?

- How would this same priority for love expressed in 1 Corinthians 13 transfer to your marriage?

Remember…To LOVE your mate is a conscious CHOICE you must make every day.

To love or not love—that is the question!

Action to Keep Attraction

What actions will you and your spouse take to incorporate into your marriage the principles, practices, and lessons learned in this chapter? Write out your goals, plans, and strategies to achieve them on the lines below.

_____

_____

_____

_____

_____

_____

_____

_____

_____

_____

_____

_____

_____

_____

A Prayer for Your Marriage

Heavenly Father, I come praying for the healing and restoration of hurt, broken, and failed marriages as a result of *conditional love* and *unforgiving hearts.* Holy Spirit, speak to the hearts of husbands and wives, flooding them with the overwhelming desire to restore and reclaim their broken marriage so they once again represent Christ's love for the church.

Lord, penetrate their hearts with *selflessness, forgiveness,* and *unconditional love* for one another and give them humble spirits so their lifestyles will line up with your WORD, and their prayers may be heard.

It's in Jesus' mighty, matchless, and miraculous name I pray. Amen.

Have You Invested in The Health of Your Marriage TODAY?

Prayer for HIS/HER Heart

A Personal Prayer for Your Spouse and Marriage

Heavenly Father,

_____

_____

_____

_____

_____

_____

_____

_____

_____

_____

_____

_____

_____

_____

Day Eleven

Praying Together to Stay Together

Do not be anxious about anything, but in every situation, by prayer and petition, with thanksgiving, present your requests to God. And the peace of God, which transcends all understanding, will guard your hearts and your minds in Christ Jesus.

Philippians 4:6-7 (NIV)

PRAYING TOGETHER CAN GIVE birth to a *REVIVAL* in your marriage. Whether your marriage is great, on a respirator, or it has flat lined—PRAYER WORKS when all else fails! GOD is still on his throne, and he reigns with complete sovereignty. There is NO burden too heavy for Jesus to bear—NO pain he cannot heal—and NO storm he cannot still...when you *PRAY!*

While my husband James and I were dating, he developed the habit of regularly giving me intimate cards that expressed his love for me or sending emails or texts that shared how he felt about our relationship. After marriage, he continued to give me intimate cards (with his words of affection inscribed inside) and sending emails/texts. But he also began leaving me little *"love notes"* around the house in places he knew I would visit before the day or night was over—like on the bathroom mirror, my nightstand, or on my pillow. He did this because he saw from the beginning how much *joy* these little *"acts of love"* brought me. Then, he began to extend these love notes to include *"love prayers."* For example, one time when I was out of town on a business trip, he sent me the follow prayer.

August 29, 2011 @ 11:06 PM

My Baby, here is my Prayer for you tonight.

Dear Lord,

Thank you for this blessed day you've given us. We have our health, strength, and life in you. Thank you for Mary—you blessed her with a heart to praise you. God, her love for you is so wonderful. Thank you, Father, for giving her traveling grace. She is your Woman of God. Bless her tonight as she rests away from home. Please give her comfort and a good night's sleep. Let her know and feel your presence as she's away. Bless her to awake to a new day in you, Lord. Let her know that I miss her and I will be praying for her peace all night while here at work. Thank you, Lord, for giving me such a precious gift in Mary. Please bring her safely back to me tomorrow night. Thank you for the love we have one for another. Continue to grow us and use us for your kingdom. Thank you, God, for my Beloved. In her I delight. Thank you for putting such a passion for her in my heart that I never want to be without her. I love Mary with all my heart. You've shown me how to love her by your example of loving the Church. Help me, dear Father, in all of my ways and give me the proper decision-making ability in order to make the right choices for our lives. Lead me to the right day job so I can spend the nights with the One I Love. Father, continue to bless Mary with your wisdom and guidance as she leads the Prayer Ministry at church. Bless her to be the godly wife she is to me. Bless our marriage to stay strong in you. Thank you for having a praying wife in my life. I need Mary probably more than she needs me. Thank you for letting me be her blessed husband. May your will be done in Mary's life—I love her! It's in Jesus' name I pray. Amen.

I Luv U Honey.

P.S. I have a big hug and kiss waiting on you when you get home!

Now, some may think this letter is a little sappy. To each his own. But it was exactly what I needed at the time. August 29th is my deceased mother's birthday, and no matter how long she has been gone to her heavenly home,

I still miss her miserably not being here with us. I was having a particularly difficult day with me being away from home alone, so after my husband and I prayed together over the phone, he later emailed me this *"love prayer"* in which he poured out his heart to me and to God.

Many people pray for many different things when it comes to praying for a spouse. Often husbands and wives find it difficult to pray out loud with their spouse and be totally honest and transparent in their prayers. If this is the case for you and your spouse, you might consider incorporating writing *"love prayers"* into your marriage. If you are not quite sure how to get started, below is a simple, but effective prayer plan for your spouse that can be used verbally or in writing love prayers.

A Simple, but Effective Prayer Plan for Your Spouse

Spiritual Desires—Pray that he/she:

- Loves God with all their heart, soul, and mind.

- Lives a saved, sanctified and filled with the Holy Spirit lifestyle–equally yoked.

- Loves you just for who and whose you are—more than just skin-deep love, but love that is unconditional.

- Becomes or continues active involvement in ministry, including active in the local church, so that they may operate in and use their spiritual gifts to serve God's people and further kingdom building work.

- Is a true man or woman of God by God's definition—surrendering to God's ultimate leadership.

- Has a fervent praying spirit and loves to praise and worship the Lord!

Emotional/Relational Desires—Pray that he/she:

- Has no *"emotional baggage"* (that they have not checked at the

Lord's alter) from previous relationships that will hinder or stunt your growth in oneness and love for one another.

- Will be patient; slow to anger; quick to forgive; and do not hold grudges or seek vengeance.

- Will be a loving spouse and parent, if children are involved. The family will intertwine and become one in mutual love and respect for each other.

- Will agree to put each other first and most important in priority in relationship to *ALL* other family members, in accordance with God's divine order.

- Will be equally yoked with you in life, as well as in the bedroom, and in the prayer room!

Financial Desires—Pray that he/she:

- Be financially stable with good credit, untainted spending habits and adequate life insurance, etc. Be willing to help your mate build good credit, including a household budget prepared in agreement.

- Maintains limited debt and has wisdom in managing money and using credit wisely.

- Has the same goals, values, and desires as it pertains to material things, e.g. money management, savings, investments, home ownership, insurance, etc., as well as spiritual things.

Physical Desires—Pray that he/she:

- Will know how to laugh and make you laugh. They can be serious, when necessary, but also know how to have fun—*PRAY* and *PLAY TOGETHER!*

- Is sensitive and romantic—knows when to give gifts, be spontaneous, share affirmation, or simply knows when to cuddle and/or quietly hold you in their arms.

- Always remains attractive to you and vice versa—both inside and outside!

"HE"

You have stolen my heart, my sister, my bride; you have stolen my heart with one glance of your eyes, with one jewel of your necklace.

Song of Solomon 4:9

"SHE"

Awake, north wind, and come, south wind! Blow on my garden, that its fragrance may spread everywhere. Let my beloved come into his garden and taste its choice fruits.

Song of Solomon 4:16

Action to Keep Attraction

What actions will you and your spouse take to incorporate into your marriage the principles, practices, and lessons learned in this chapter? Write out your goals, plans, and strategies to achieve them on the lines below.

_____

_____

_____

_____

_____

_____

_____

_____

_____

_____

_____

_____

_____

_____

_____

A Prayer for Your Marriage

Heavenly Father, I pray that you will raise up and restore Christian marriages, so they truly reflect Christ's love for the Church. For we know divorce is not your will, but rather for man and wife to grow as one together in love and harmony. Bless this husband and wife with forgiving hearts and a desire to do marriage "God's way" and not their own way.

Help this husband to love you with his whole heart and love his wife like Christ loves the church. Bless and enable this husband to be the provider, godly head of household, divine leader, and loving and affectionate priest of his home.

I pray this wife will support, encourage, respect, and humbly submit to her husband, as unto the Lord, with joy; and trust the God in her husband to lead as Christ would have him lead.

Help both mates to commit to praying together daily and to consistently study God's Word together to cultivate an atmosphere of love, respect, unity, forgiveness, and peace in their home.

Father GOD, allow oneness, commitment, and unconditional love to rule and reign over and within this marriage, keeping the sanctity of the marriage bed pure as unto the Lord. Most of all, LORD, let selflessness and forgiveness be abundant and allow this couple to show humility of spirit in all they do so their prayers may not be hindered.

Thank you, Father, for healing and restoring broken marriages and for blessing and uplifting this marriage. It's In Jesus' mighty, matchless, and miraculous name I pray! Amen.

Have You Invested in The Health of Your Marriage TODAY?

Prayer for HIS/HER Heart

A Personal Prayer for Your Spouse and Marriage

Heavenly Father,

_____

_____

_____

_____

_____

_____

_____

_____

_____

_____

_____

_____

_____

_____

_____

_____

Day Twelve

Can You Hear Me Now?

Let the husband render to his wife the affection due her, and likewise also the wife to her husband.

1 Corinthians 7:3

THERE HAVE BEEN MANY good books written about effective communication and learning to speak your spouse's *"love language"* to grow closer in oneness together. But, if we are honest with ourselves, what we perceive as effective communication in marriage is when we can get our point across with the goal of *"being heard,"* which does not always lead to *"being understood."* In addition, many husbands and wives have not seriously considered that their spouse may be *"bilingual"* when it comes to love languages, depending on what they are going through or dealing with at that point in time.

This desert place in spousal communication leads to gaps in the marital relationship. As a result, divorce due to irreconcilable differences becomes the scapegoat for many couples. However, I would recommend that before you harbor the thought of changing spouses, consider changing the love language instead. Even though most women and men do want basic things from their spouses (see previous chapters 4-5), there are some specific things each of us wants from our spouse to feel we are deeply loved and truly heard and understood in the marital relationship. The best and easiest way to find out exactly what your spouse wants and needs within the marriage is to... *simply ask!* Set aside a special time when you and your spouse can honestly share what is on your heart... not what's on your mind.

Heart-to-Heart is a time for genuine gut-level sharing between a husband and wife. This is a time when you and your spouse can get sincerely honest with each other about who you are and what's happening in your lives. In this atmosphere you can share hurts, reveal pain points, openly and honestly bare your feelings to each other, confess your failures, disclose your doubts, admit your fears, acknowledge your weaknesses, and ask each other for help and forgiveness. After each of you have bared your souls and stand completely "naked" *(figuratively or literally)* before each other... go to GOD together in prayer. Pray one at a time and pray for specific needs shared during the heart-to-heart. Don't delay... get started today.

Heart-2-Heart

When was the last time you had a real heart-to-heart with your spouse? Well, that's too long! Be intentional and set aside at least an hour (or more) of uninterrupted time to spend with your spouse alone. That means <u>no</u> TV, radio, music, cell phone, children, family, or friends to interrupt your dedicated time together. During this heart-to-heart time, the wife will talk first and the *husband will listen only*. Then the husband will take his turn to talk, and the *wife will listen only*.

When it's your time to talk, you will need to be *open* and *honest* with your spouse and *tell him/her exactly what you want and need from him/her as your husband/wife.* If what you need, they are already giving to you, then this is the perfect time to let them know this and tell them how you feel about it—***share your heart!*** But if there is something you need from them they are not currently giving to you—*then tell them what it is and why you need it from them*—***share your heart!***

Remember... you must not interrupt, criticize, analyze, antagonize, or try to renegotiate with your spouse while he/she is talking and sharing their heart. **Your assignment is to *only listen—but listen with your HEART.***

The husband should give his wife what she deserves as his wife. And the wife should give her husband what he deserves as her husband.

1 Corinthians 7:3 (ERV)

Action to Keep Attraction

What actions will you and your spouse take to incorporate into your marriage the principles, practices, and lessons learned in this chapter? Write out your goals, plans, and strategies to achieve them on the lines below.

_____

_____

_____

_____

_____

_____

_____

_____

_____

_____

_____

_____

_____

A Prayer for Your Marriage

Heavenly Father, your Word says in James 1:17 that "Every good gift and every perfect gift is from above, coming down from the father of lights, with whom there is no variation or shadow due to change." You, Oh Lord, have ordained marriage as one of those good and perfect gifts. Thank you for your righteous right hand that will hold us up, cover, protect, and guide this couple safely into your promises for their marriage. For we know that even in the midnight hour, you can and will turn it all around to work in their favor!

Father GOD, help this couple to hold on to your unchanging hand and faint not, nor get weary with doing well, because that which was sent by the enemy to destroy their marriage is NOW working in their favor!

Thank you, ABBA, for your faithfulness to perfect and fulfill every promise for their marriage. It's in the mighty and matchless name of Jesus I pray and praise forever. Amen.

Have You Invested in The Health of Your Marriage TODAY?

Prayer for HIS/HER Heart

A Personal Prayer for Your Spouse and Marriage

Heavenly Father,

_____

_____

_____

_____

_____

_____

_____

_____

_____

_____

_____

_____

_____

_____

Day Thirteen

Covenant Keepers—Made to Last!

The man said, 'This is now bone of my bones and flesh of my flesh; she shall be called "woman," for she was taken out of man.' That is why a man leaves his father and mother and is united to his wife, and they become one flesh.

Genesis 2:23-24 (NIV)

God designed marriage to be a tangible representation of Christ's love for The Church. In the beginning, He created one man for one woman. This was (and still is) a *covenant relationship* between a man and a woman *with GOD* himself—not simply a "contract" between the man and woman that can be broken upon mutual consent. This unified oneness was made to last a lifetime *in covenant with GOD* (Genesis 2:24).

As you live out your marriage in covenant with God, expect GOD to faithfully fulfill every promise He has given for marriage. In turn, setting you free to live as you *should* in your marriage with *oneness* in mind, and not simply live to please your fleshly desires. The covenant of marriage requires that we lay down our lifelong commitment to *ourselves* for the greater good of the one to whom we pledged our oath before our holy GOD to honor, love, and care for... *"until death do us part."*

However, too often we rely upon our intellect, emotional feelings, and even faulty advice from friends and family to help resolve marital issues. But GOD's Word is the Christian's blueprint to help us live out His promises in our lives, including through the sacred bond of marriage. Just remember, God can do more speaking to your spouse's *heart* than you can do shouting at their *head*. Where intellect fails, GOD's grace prevails!

> *"Let us then with confidence draw near to the throne of grace, that we may receive mercy and find grace to help in time of need."*
>
> Hebrews 4:16

As you strive to walk in lifelong oneness and unconditional love with your spouse, I encourage you to read and meditate often upon I Corinthians 13. This chapter is sometimes called the *love chapter* because it outlines God's expectations for his children to have an *excellent love*. Let's look closely at a few verses from this love chapter to see how, when properly applied, these golden nuggets can help reignite the flames of passion and fortify your marriage, especially when it becomes weakened.

> *"Though I speak with the tongues of men and of angels, but have not love, I have become sounding brass or a clanging cymbal. And though I have the gift of prophecy, and understand all mysteries and all knowledge, and though I have all faith, so that I could remove mountains, but have not love, I am nothing. And though I bestow all my goods to feed the poor, and though I give my body to be burned, but have not love, it profits me nothing. Love suffers long and is kind; love does not envy; love does not parade itself, is not puffed up; does not behave rudely, does not seek its own, is not provoked, thinks no evil; does not rejoice in iniquity, but rejoices in the truth; bears all things, believes all things, hopes all things, endures all things. Love never fails."*
>
> 1 Corinthians 13: 1-4

LOVE IS PATIENT. The art of practicing patience has been lost to many in this age of "hurry up and wait!" Instead of worrying your spouse to death, try loving them to life! Although this may test your patience from time to time, you must commit to practice loving each other unconditionally—daily. Seeking to love your spouse every day in a manner that pleases God will open new insight and revelation of how God so patiently loves you beyond your faults each day. This epiphany will cause you to extend grace to your spouse, just as God extends grace to you. *"Beloved, let us love one another, for love is of God, and everyone who loves is born of God and knows God."* (1 John 4:7).

LOVE MAKES YOU KIND. Kindness is a characteristic of a loving spouse—no matter the circumstances. Just because *"it's true"* doesn't mean *"its kind"* to say or display. Kindness is how *love acts* to create a positive outcome—it's really love in action! *"And be kind to one another, tenderhearted, forgiving one another, even as God in Christ forgave you."* (Ephesians 4:32).

LOVE DOES NOT ENVY. When you understand the concept of marital oneness, then you can freely support your spouse without the feelings of inadequacy, jealousy, or competition. Instead of being envious, try doing what is needed at the moment it is needed—cooperate and accommodate—not dictate! Generosity kills a covetous spirit. *"And let us not grow weary while doing good, for in due season we shall reap if we do not lose heart."* (Galatians 6:9).

LOVE IS NOT PRIDEFUL. You may say if it's true, it's no brag—just facts! Well, if you are the only one always stating the *"facts"* about yourself, it could become a big drag for everyone else around you—including your spouse. On the other side of that coin, don't let saying the two little words of *"I'm sorry"* or *"forgive me"* cause you to choke—especially when they could mean the difference between divorce or *"happily ever after."* Just remember, pride comes before a fall, and arrogance is the one who made you trip. *"Then Peter came to Jesus and asked, 'Lord, how many times shall I forgive my brother when he sins against me? Up to seven times?' Jesus answered, 'I tell you, not seven times, but seventy-seven times.'"* (Matthew 18:21-22).

LOVE IS NOT SELFISH. Although selfishness is a part of human nature, it is the opposite of love. God gives the gift of *"selflessness"* to those who truly strive to demonstrate love—especially in marriage. Selflessness creates inner joy and breeds devotion to your spouse. As opposed to looking out for your good, you begin to focus on what is good for your spouse and your marriage. When you learn to say "*no*" to your selfish wants and "*yes*" to your spouse's needs, it cultivates a marriage full of devotion, dedication, and honor. True love looks for ways to say yes! *"Do nothing out of selfish ambition or vain conceit. Rather, in humility value others above yourselves, not looking to your own interests, but each of you to the interests of the others."* (Philippians 2:3-4).

LOVE IS THOUGHTFUL, NOT RUDE. _Thoughtlessness_ can be a silent killer to a vibrant and loving relationship between husband and wife. Simply put, *"think before you speak"*—engage your mind before you pull the trigger on your lips. Genuine love is not rude—so, mind your manners and be polite; there is always a better way to say something if just given a little thought. Even when it's much easier to *"speak your mind,"* don't—instead listen with your heart. Love always requires you to rise to a higher standard—God's standard. *"He who blesses his neighbor with a loud voice early in the morning, it will be counted as a curse to him [for it will either be annoying or his purpose will be suspect]."* (Proverbs 27:14 AMP).

This Marriage is Made to LAST!

Action to Keep Attraction

What actions will you and your spouse take to incorporate into your marriage the principles, practices, and lessons learned in this chapter? Write out your goals, plans, and strategies to achieve them on the lines below.

_____

_____

_____

_____

_____

_____

_____

_____

_____

_____

_____

_____

_____

_____

_____

_____

A Prayer for Your Marriage

Heavenly Father, I come praying for this couple and all marriages around the world. According to your Word, you designed marriage to be a tangible representation of Christ's love for the Church. Therefore, I decree and declare that three cords are not easily broken when the enemy comes into our homes and into our marriages to KILL LOVE, STEAL JOY and PEACE, and DESTROY the COVENANT of godly marriages!

Father God, help us place our attention, affection, and desires on pleasing our mates and not on our selfish wants. For your Word, Oh Lord, has the solution to every problem, the cure for any malfunction, the comfort needed for the broken-hearted, and it provides peace that passes all understanding even in the midst of the most difficult situations.

Thank you, ABBA, for being loving, merciful and never failing—you are indeed faithful! It's in the Name above every name, JESUS, I pray and praise you always! Amen!

> *"And we have known and believed the love that God has for us. God is love, and he who abides in love abides in God, and God in him."*
>
> I John 4:16

Have You Invested in The Health of Your Marriage TODAY?

Prayer for HIS/HER Heart

A Personal Prayer for Your Spouse and Marriage

Heavenly Father,

_____

_____

_____

_____

_____

_____

_____

_____

_____

_____

_____

_____

_____

_____

Day Fourteen

Dating Your Mate

Like a lily among thorns is my darling among the young women. Like an apple tree among the trees of the forest is my beloved among the young men. I delight to sit in his shade, and his fruit is sweet to my taste.

Song of Solomon 2:2-3

IT WAS ONCE SAID to me about marriage, *"Don't start nothing that you're not willing to keep up."* Failing to adhere to this sound advice has caused many a marriage to suffer from *"withdrawals"* after one mate (or both) decides it is no longer necessary to continue the *"love practices"* they did while dating. But remember this... the same things it took to catch your mate will be the same things (plus more) it will take to keep your marriage!

I remember when I started dating my husband prior to marriage. Our first date was a five-and-a-half-hour brunch date neither of us anticipated would last more than an hour or so. It's a long story I'll save for another time, but the conversation and unguarded openness was like a breath of fresh air for us both.

During the courtship, and into the first several months of our marriage, I remember sharing with a friend how my new husband was always so attentive, making sure I felt like I was the only one in the room when we were together, and he always brought me flowers. My friend had been married for several years and her response was, *"You're still in the honeymoon stage of your marriage, so don't be surprised when the newness wears off."*

Well, it's been over eighteen years of marriage, and my husband continues to be the perfect gentleman—opens doors for me, pulls out my chair, takes me out to dinner, and he still brings me candy and flowers on more than just special occasions. And, of course, I reciprocate with all the little things I know he loves as well. These and many other little *love practices* didn't stop once we said, *"I DO."*

The longer you are married, the more you will find it takes *"intentionality"* to keep your mate in their rightful #2 spot—only after Christ being #1. Not your parents, children, friends, or ministry. Be very intentional about *"keeping the home fire burning"* in your marriage by continuing to practice the things your spouse desires—*like date nights.*

Why *"date your mate"* after the wedding? Simply put, what it took to *"catch them"* will be what it will take to *"keep them."* Date nights send a signal to your spouse (and to family and friends) that you consider them to still be the most important person in your life (other than Christ); so much that you intentionally set aside special time to spend with them—on a regular basis. Date nights foster a sense of togetherness, sets the atmosphere for meaningful communication, and promotes intimacy and oneness in marriage. Let's look at some simple steps to dating your spouse.

- **Make the Time.** The first step to dating your spouse is to be committed to making the time to date them—no matter what! Warning... this might not sit well with family, friends, and even your ministry. They may even attempt to stray you away from designated "date nights" as if it were not as important as what they want you to do with them. Stand your ground! Remind them you have a date—don't break your date.

- **Have Heart-to-Hearts.** Sometimes, select date spots where you can have a meaningful conversation with your spouse. Communication, along with sex and money, is one of the top three reasons marriages go south. Couples drift apart, and the next thing you know, you are living with a stranger. People change over the years, so keep up with those changes.

- **Get Creative.** Have date nights in the daylight. You don't always have to wait until the weekend or a pre-designated time and day to spend quality time on a date with your spouse. Meet your spouse at their workplace and take them out for lunch or pack a picnic basket and meet them on the patio for a late supper, or... I believe you get the idea. Be creative!

- **Together is Better.** Do things together with your spouse more than you do things with your friends. Your spouse should never have to feel they are in competition with others for your attention. Be sexy for your spouse—sometimes sexy has to override comfort.

- **Get-a-way with your Bae.** You don't always have to go broke for a date or spend money you don't have on long vacations and trips around the world. This will only put undue financial pressure on your marriage. Going on short get-a-ways for the weekend or doing staycations (if the money is funny) can still allow the needed time together without the everyday worries and responsibilities. Remember... if you are unhappy with your spouse at home, then you will be unhappy with them on another continent. It's not the place; it's the person you're with that makes the difference!

Don't let the honeymoon stage of marriage fade into the distance—fan the flames by dating your mate!

Action to Keep Attraction

What actions will you and your spouse take to incorporate into your marriage the principles, practices, and lessons learned in this chapter? Write out your goals, plans, and strategies to achieve them on the lines below.

_____

_____

_____

_____

_____

_____

_____

_____

_____

_____

_____

_____

_____

_____

A Prayer for Your Marriage

Heavenly Father, I stand in agreement with this couple for their marriage. As your beloved children, we come declaring that Satan can't have what YOU have already blessed and ordained... our marriages!

Father GOD, cover this marriage in the sanctifying blood of Jesus—restore that which the locust has eaten. Make NEW that which has worn old. Resurrect that which appeared dead. Send your fire and desire back into the hearts of this husband and wife, even if they thought they had no hope.

SATAN... YOU'VE BEEN SERVED NOTICE! WE CLAIM VICTORY IN EVERY AREA UNDER ATTACK IN THIS MARRIAGE. GLORIFY YOURSELF FATHER. IN JESUS' MOST POWERFUL NAME. AMEN!

Have You Invested in the Health of Your Marriage TODAY?

Prayer for HIS/HER Heart

A Personal Prayer for Your Spouse and Marriage

Heavenly Father,

_____

_____

_____

_____

_____

_____

_____

_____

_____

_____

_____

_____

_____

_____

_____

Day Fifteen

The Ministry of a Praying Husband

By Rev. James A. Ford, Jr.

Now Isaac pleaded with the Lord for his wife, because she was barren; and the Lord granted his plea, and Rebekah his wife conceived.

Genesis 25:21 (NAS95)

You husbands in the same way, live with your wives in an understanding way, as with someone weaker, since she is a woman; and show her honor as a fellow heir of the grace of life, so that your prayers will not be hindered.

1Peter 3:7 (NAS95)

ARE YOU TRULY PRAYING for your mate?

When one reads these two passages of scripture about a husband's prayer, care, and love for his wife, one often wonders why husbands don't pray for their wives more. You see, these two scriptures remind me of how important it is to pray for my wife. And to pray for my marriage and family. If I don't do it, as the head of my household, I leave my covering over them off, and they are now even more vulnerable to the enemy's attack on their lives.

I think we men often forget how powerful our prayers are to God. You see, when Isaac prayed for his wife, it was not about controlling her or having his way over her. It was from his deep love for his wife. During that time in history, society looked down upon a wife that could not have children. It meant she had sinned, or God was punishing her for something with barrenness. However, it was not true she had committed a sin, or she was being punished by God. It was a test of God for both Rebekah and Isaac. God wanted to see just how much faith they had in him.

Now, I'm sure Rebekah prayed to God about being barren, but God did not answer. He waited until He heard from her husband. Isaac didn't just want his wife's or his will done. He wanted God's will done for their lives. *"Now this is the confidence that we have in Him, that if we ask anything according to His will, He hears us."* (1 John 5:14).

God does indeed want us to pray about everything, but He wants us to pray according to His will. That's why it's important to ask God to reveal His Will for your wife, marriage, and family, so you can pray accordingly. When Isaac prayed, God answered, because it was God's will for Rebekah to have children. Through their children, the nation of Israel would come to be. The Savior of the world would come through their family linage. So, we need to make sure when we pray, it lines up with Gods will.

Husbands, it is also important to live with our wives in an understanding way. This means treating them and loving them like the queens they are made to be in our lives. We should always be looking for what is best for our wife instead of only wanting what we can get from them. Our wife is not our property but our helpmate. She is the woman God created for us to have in life for this Christian journey. Make sure not to take your wife for granted and always pray for her. Praying for your wife will not only soften her heart toward you and the marriage, but it will also soften yours as well. No matter what has happened between you, God can fix it! He is the God of wholeness and restoration. God has given you the power and authority... so pray!

Whenever a wife hears that her husband is praying for her, it makes her feel loved and protected (covered). It makes her feel she's important to you in life. I prayed for my wife before I met her. I wanted to have the wife God wanted for me. Not just what I wanted, because I wanted God's best

blessing in a wife. I trusted and believed God would answer my prayer...
and He did!

I not only got the wife God wanted me to have but so much more. God
gave me in my wife, Mary, not just what I asked for, but so much more.
She has blessed me in so many ways I never thought or imagined I needed.
I love that God always gives us not just what we want, but what we need
in life. My wife praying for me daily is a joy to my soul. Being able to do
ministry together has been one of the greatest joys of my marriage to her.
She is my best friend and my prayer partner. Wow! What a blessing from
God.

~THINK ABOUT IT~

Are you wondering, *"how can I pray for my wife more effectively?"* I
would say seek God for the answer—pray about it. He made her, and He
knows exactly what she needs. When you pray, look for God to reveal
opportunities to pray for your wife in specific ways. You will then see
blessings flow because *you prayed for her!*

Think about the following questions and how you can include your
answers into your personal prayer time for your wife.

1. How often do you pray *for* your wife? Does she ever *hear* you pray
   for her?

2. Have you specifically prayed for your marriage and asked God to
   help you *become one* with your wife?

3. Do you pray for your wife's *spiritual* growth?

4. Have you asked your wife, *"How can l pray for you?"*

5. What are some *hindrances* stopping you from praying *with* your
   wife?

6. What is your *motivation* for praying *for* your wife?

Action to Keep Attraction

What actions will you take to incorporate into your marriage the principles, practices, and lessons learned in this chapter? Write down on the lines below your specific answers to the "Think About It" questions and include the things that can help you pray more effectively for your wife.

_____

_____

_____

_____

_____

_____

_____

_____

_____

_____

_____

_____

_____

_____

A Prayer for Your Marriage

Father God, thank you for creating marriage. You made wives to be a complement to husbands, and to make us complete. You do the same for wives. I pray you will make this couple as one.

Lord, give this husband a heart of compassion toward his wife and the patience to listen to her when she needs him to do so. Father God, increase this husband's love for his wife and enable him to show her his love in a way that makes her more beautiful to him.

I pray this prayer in Jesus' Name. Amen!

"Therefore, a man shall leave his father and mother and be joined to his wife, and they shall become one flesh. And they were both naked, the man and his wife, and were not ashamed." (Genesis 2:24-25).

Have You Invested in The Health of Your Marriage TODAY?

Prayer for HIS/HER Heart

A Personal Prayer for Your Spouse and Marriage

Heavenly Father,

_____

_____

_____

_____

_____

_____

_____

_____

_____

_____

_____

_____

_____

_____

Day Sixteen

The Ministry of a Praying Wife

Be alert and of sober mind. Your enemy the devil prowls around like a roaring lion looking for someone to devour.

1 Peter 5:8

As wives, we have seen our husbands in the best of times and in the worst of times. We have been there when they were feeling on top of the mountain and when the mountain seemed to be on top of them. Wives have unmatched access to our husbands, which allows us to see them even in their most vulnerable state. We have inside knowledge those on the outside do not have. So who is better able to pray for our husbands than us?

It's no secret that most men do not always or easily share their most deep feelings—especially when it comes to their emotions of inadequacy, frustration, fear, and failure. This is why it is vitally important to always pray for your husband—daily. Most tend to pray only when things are going astray, but as Christian wives, we should get into the spiritual habit of praying daily for our husbands—rain or shine.

Why pray for your husband even when things are going well? Because as the Priest of your home, your husband is on the front line in spiritual warfare against an enemy that doesn't play fair or take prisoners—Satan. *"Be alert and of sober mind. Your enemy the devil prowls around like a roaring lion looking for someone to devour."* (1 Peter 5:8).

Satan thrives in chaos, and he is constantly seeking ways to insert it into your marriage. No matter what chaos or confusion the enemy has launched against your husband or your marriage—poor health, devastating disease, fatal finances, unhealthy work habits, fickle friends, fractured marriage vows, or dysfunctional family—even in the eye of your storm, you can still experience God's calm. Prayer muzzles the mouth of the enemy and takes the bite out of Satan's bark. After all, a muzzled dog can't bite!

I thank God for the ministry of a praying wife. Praying for your husband gives you the opportunity to partner with Heaven on his behalf—even when he does not ask or does not even know how to ask for prayer. If you are not already practicing the ministry of a praying wife, then don't delay—start today!

Whether your marriage is great, on a respirator, or it has flat lined—PRAYER WORKS when all else fails. Below are a few areas of prayer to focus on when praying for your husband.

HOW TO PRAY FOR YOUR HUSBAND

1. Pray for your husband's heart to be pure and not yield to the lusts of his flesh. *"Whatever comes from [the heart of] a man, that is what defiles and dishonors him."* (Mark 7:20-22 AMP).

2. Pray for your husband to be loving and patient. *"Let everyone be quick to hear [be a careful, thoughtful listener], slow to speak [a speaker of carefully chosen words and], slow to anger [patient, reflective, forgiving]."* (James 1:19 AMP).

3. Pray for your husband to have a forgiving spirit. *"Bearing graciously with one another, and willingly forgiving each other if one has a cause for complaint against another; just as the Lord has forgiven you, so should you forgive."* (Colossians 3:13 AMP).

4. Pray for your husband's walk with Christ. *"But the fruit of the Spirit [the result of His presence within us] is love [unselfish concern for others], joy, [inner] peace, patience [not the ability*

to wait, but how we act while waiting], kindness, goodness, faithfulness, gentleness, self-control. Against such things there is no law." (Galatians 5:22-23 AMP).

5. Pray for your husband's mind and battle against temptation. *"Set your mind and keep focused habitually on the things above [the heavenly things], not on things that are on the earth [which have only temporal value]."* (Colossians 3:2 AMP).

6. Pray for your husband's decision making and wisdom. *"For those who are living according to the flesh set their minds on the things of the flesh [which gratify the body], but those who are living according to the Spirit, [set their minds on] the things of the Spirit [His will and purpose]."* (Romans 8:5-6 AMP).

7. Pray for your husband's role as "husband" in the marriage. *"For the husband is head of the wife, as Christ is head of the church, Himself being the Savior of the body."* (Ephesians 5:22-23 AMP).

8. Pray for your husband's physical health. *"Do you not know that your body is a temple of the Holy Spirit who is within you, whom you have [received as a gift] from God, and that you are not your own [property]? So then, honor and glorify God with your body."* (1 Corinthians 6:19-20 AMP).

9. Pray for your husband as the provider for the home—his work ethics, career advancements, and sound business practices. *"Whatever you do [whatever your task may be], work from the soul [that is, put in your very best effort], as [something done] for the Lord and not for men, knowing [with all certainty] that it is from the Lord [not from men] that you will receive the inheritance which is your [greatest] reward. It is the Lord Christ whom you [actually] serve."* (Colossians 3:23-24 AMP).

10. Pray for your husband's calling in life and ministry. *"Eye has not seen, nor ear heard, nor have entered into the heart of man the things which God has prepared for those who love Him."* (1 Corinthians 2:9).

11. Pray for your husband's fatherhood. *"And you, fathers, do not provoke your children to wrath, but bring them up in the training and admonition of the Lord."* (Ephesians 6:4).

12. Pray for your husband's relationship with others, including friends and family. *"As iron sharpens iron, so a man sharpens the countenance of his friend."* (Proverbs 27:17).

13. Pray for peace to flow freely in your marital relationship. *"If it is possible, as much as depends on you, live peaceably with all men."* (Romans 12:18).

"Watch over your heart with all diligence, for from it flow the springs of life."

Proverbs 4:23

Action to Keep Attraction

What actions will you take to incorporate into your marriage the principles, practices, and lessons learned in this chapter? Write out your goals, plans, and strategies to achieve them on the lines below.

_____

_____

_____

_____

_____

_____

_____

_____

_____

_____

_____

_____

_____

_____

A Prayer for Your Marriage

Heavenly Father, bless this husband and wife with forgiving hearts and a desire to do marriage "God's way" and not their own. Help this husband to love the Lord with his whole heart and love his wife like Christ loves the church. Bless and enable this husband to be the provider, godly head of his household, spiritual leader, and loving and affectionate priest of his own home.

Father God, help this wife to support, encourage, respect, and humbly submit to her own husband, as unto the Lord with joy, and trust the God in her husband to lead as Christ would have him to lead the family. Help this wife to commit to praying not only with her husband, but for her husband daily to help cultivate an atmosphere of love, respect, unity, and peace in their home.

Thank you, ABBA, for being a healer and restorer of broken marriages; and for blessing and binding this marriage closer in oneness through the power of prayer. Thank you for hearing and answering this prayer, in Jesus' name I pray. Amen.

Have You Invested in The Health of Your Marriage TODAY?

Prayer for HIS/HER Heart

A Personal Prayer for Your Spouse and Marriage

Heavenly Father,

_____

_____

_____

_____

_____

_____

_____

_____

_____

_____

_____

_____

_____

_____

_____

_____

Day Seventeen

You Complete Me!

Do not be unequally yoked together with unbelievers. For what fellowship has righteousness with lawlessness? And what communion has light with darkness?

2 Corinthians 6:14

THE APOSTLE PAUL WARNED the Believers of Corinth that they should not *"yoke"* (tie or bind) themselves together with unbelievers. He then used the analogy of the lack of fellowship that light has with darkness, or that Christ has with Satan. Paul was warning believers to beware of making mismatched alliances with unbelievers that are inconsistent with their faith. Just as Christ does not have fellowship or harmony with Satan, or we do not worship idols in the temple of God, believers should not have this intimate *"oneness"* with unbelievers. (2 Corinthians 6:14-17).

A yoke is what joins two animals (usually oxen) together to carry a cart (heavy load) to a specific destination. If one of the yoked oxen is pulling more in one direction than the other, well, let's just say the journey will not be easy, and they might even wind up pulling each other apart along the way.

Oftentimes, Believers overlook this warning pertaining to being *"unequally yoked"* and enter marriage with non-believers. The inequality can cause devastating strain on marriages which many times end in divorce, because two unequally yoked people—with two different beliefs and moral systems—are pulling in different directions—one pulling toward God and the other pulling away from Him.

However, an equally yoked relationship is not one just united by your faith, but also united in mind, heart, and spirit—*oneness!* Just like the two oxen pulling the cart together to accomplish the same goal—they arrive at the same destination with load intact. So it is with the husband and wife in a marital relationship. Being equally yoked means both are committed to growing, maturing, and working together in concert with God to accomplish the same end—*fulfilling God's calling on their life and becoming more like Christ.*

But does being unequally yoked only pertain to whether you are a Christian or non-Christian when it comes to marriage? Can being unequally yoked happen even in a Christian home with both husband and wife being Believers? Yes, it can. After all, two professing Christians are still two broken human beings with the *free will* to seek God more intimately—or not to.

When dating your potential spouse, the most important question to ask and confirm is, *"Are you a Christian?"* If the answer is *"no,"* then you might want to quickly rethink any further pursuit of the relationship unless you are able to lead them to Christ prior to marriage. The next question to ask is, *"Will this person help or hinder me in reaching my God-ordained calling in life as I grow more and more like Christ?"* These are essential questions to ask and prayerfully ponder when seeking a lifelong mate that *completes you* in marriage—*your bookend for life!*

God made you different from your spouse so that you *complete* each other. Godly marriage is all about *oneness—feeling complete.* Loving your *"we time"* more than you love your *"me time"* is a sure sign of growing in oneness together. You worship God when you love and sacrifice for your spouse. Remember... marriage is like two people rowing a boat *(or pulling a cart)*—they both must work together to arrive at the desired destination and still be intact. *"Accept one another, then, just as Christ accepted you, in order to bring praise to God." Romans 15:7 (NIV).*

Action to Keep Attraction

What actions will you and your spouse take to incorporate into your marriage the principles, practices, and lessons learned in this chapter? Write out your goals, plans, and strategies to achieve them on the lines below.

_____

_____

_____

_____

_____

_____

_____

_____

_____

_____

_____

_____

_____

_____

_____

A Prayer for Your Marriage

Heavenly Father, raise up Christian marriages as a reflection of Christ's love for the Church. Father, allow oneness, unity, commitment, and unconditional love to rule and reign over and within this marriage. Lord, keep the sanctity of the marriage bed pure as unto the Lord; and allow your calling on their lives to bloom and blossom into your pre-ordained plan.

Most of all, let selflessness and forgiveness be abundant and allow this couple to show humility of spirit in all they do so their prayers may not be hindered.

Thank you, Father, for hearing and answering this humble prayer. It's in Jesus' name I pray. Amen.

Have You Invested in The Health of Your Marriage TODAY?

Prayer for HIS/HER Heart

A Personal Prayer for Your Spouse and Marriage

Heavenly Father,

_____

_____

_____

_____

_____

_____

_____

_____

_____

_____

_____

_____

_____

_____

_____

Day Eighteen
Marriage Is Ministry

For the husband is the head of the wife, as Christ also is the head of the church, He Himself being the Savior of the body. But as the church is subject to Christ, so also the wives ought to be to their husbands in everything. Husbands, love your wives, just as Christ also loved the church and gave Himself up for her, so that He might sanctify her, having cleansed her by the washing of water with the word, that He might present to Himself the church in all her glory, having no spot or wrinkle or any such thing; but that she would be holy and blameless.
Ephesians 5:23-27 (NAS95)

WHEN MOST THINK ABOUT *"ministry,"* they often think about missionary work, pastoring a church, or devoting yourself to praying, preaching, and teaching in the local church or in a specific arena. Although these are all vital aspects of the ministry of Jesus Christ, to which all Christians are called, we often don't consider *"marriage"* as being ministry. This could be because many people enter marriage for all sorts of reasons other than what God intended—to be a representation of Christ's unconditional love. As a result, this can cause the marriage vows to become a burden to uphold instead of a joy to experience, and the proclamation of *"until death do us part"* becomes a prison sentence rather than the marital haven God intended.

Marriage does matter to God. He designed it as a representation of Christ's love for the church. *"Just as Christ also loved the church and gave Himself up for her."* This means we in turn should also give ourselves up daily *(practice selflessness versus selfishness)* for the good of our spouse. This makes marriage not only a ministry, but the most important ministry a husband and wife can be involved in while here on planet earth. Yes, ministering to the lost, the church body, our children, and our family and friends is important, but they do not take precedence over ministering to our spouse.

We are saved to serve. After salvation, we are to serve others—just like Christ. However, serving is the opposite of our natural human instincts or desires. Most of the time we're more interested in 'being served' rather than serving others. But as we grow in spiritual maturity (Christlikeness), the focus of our lives should gradually shift to living a life of service—seeking "whose needs can I meet" rather than "who is going to meet my needs."

When we said "I do" to marriage, we signed up for an amazing ministry opportunity and responsibility. The unity and oneness of a husband and wife is a powerful force in the natural and spiritual realm. Marriage God's way is based upon a sacrificial love—what we can give to the relationship and not just a selfish kind of love that only seeks what we can get out of the relationship. The more we submit to (serve) one another in marriage—seeking what is best for our spouse—all needs are met, and the marriage becomes stronger. *"Submit to one another out of reverence for Christ."* (Ephesians 5:21.

Marriage is ministry, and there are many various ways we can minister to our spouses within the confines of marriage. Because God created marriage, we must consult him often through His blueprint (the Bible) and through prayer to have a healthy, fulfilling, and successful marriage. A couple that sincerely prays together stays together, and a match made in Heaven is unbreakable here on earth. When a couple freely commits to praying together daily, they invite Christ into not only their prayers, but into every aspect of their marriage. When Christ is the third cord in our marriage, it cannot be easily broken! Ask yourself this question, *"What is my marriage bound together with?"*

"And though one can overpower him who is alone, two can resist him. A cord of three strands is not quickly broken."

Ecclesiastes 4:12 (AMP)

PERSONAL NOTE—MINISTRY IN ACTION

While my husband and I spent quality time together one night, I shared with him some things weighing on my heart. Not only did he give me affectionate attention through listening that I needed so much, but he also shared a portion of God's Word that spoke directly to my concerns and redirected my thoughts to the sovereignty of our savior.

He then said, *"Honey, God has done it before, and He will do it again!"*

My husband then led us into prayer and invited our Abba Father to work in and out the situation. Immediately, the overwhelming feeling that concerned me was released and replaced with God's PEACE. The next day, I was still feeling and walking in God's overwhelming peace, breath-taking love, and unfailing grace. My soul rejoiced and my spirit shouted a resounding, *"YES LORD!"* God's peace truly does surpass all understanding! Oh, how I praise and thank God for the ministry of a praying husband, who is the priest of our home.

"Be devoted to one another in brotherly love; give preference to one another in honor."

Romans 12:10 (NAS95)

Action to Keep Attraction

What actions will you and your spouse take to incorporate into your marriage the principles, practices, and lessons learned in this chapter? Write out your goals, plans, and strategies to achieve them on the lines below.

_____

_____

_____

_____

_____

_____

_____

_____

_____

_____

_____

_____

_____

_____

_____

A Prayer for Your Marriage

Heavenly Father, allow oneness, unity, commitment, and unconditional love to rule and reign over and within this marriage. Keep the sanctity of the marriage bed pure, as unto the Lord, and most of all, let selflessness and forgiveness be abundant. Allow this couple to show humility of spirit in all they do so their prayers may not be hindered and their marriage will glorify you, the Creator.

Encourage this couple when they get weak and weary from this life's journey and renew their minds so they think of their marriage as a God sent ministry—holy and right in your sight. Consecrate this husband and wife's heart so their desires line up with your will. Help the husband to be the Priest of his home and this wife to be submissive to her husband—all to your glory and honor.

Purge their hearts from those things of the world, lusts of the flesh, and pride of this life that will hinder their witness for Christ and derail the work of their marriage ministry. It's in the mighty and matchless Name above every name, JESUS, I pray! Amen.

Have You Invested in the Health of Your Marriage TODAY?

Prayer for HIS/HER Heart

A Personal Prayer for Your Spouse and Marriage

Heavenly Father,

_____

_____

_____

_____

_____

_____

_____

_____

_____

_____

_____

_____

_____

_____

Day Nineteen
When a Man Loves a Woman

(From Trash to Treasure)
Rev. James A. Ford, Jr

Then the Lord said to me, "Go again, love a woman who is loved by her husband, yet an adulteress, even as the Lord loves the sons of Israel, though they turn to other gods and love raisin cakes." So I bought her for myself for fifteen shekels of silver and a homer and a half of barley. Then I said to her, "You shall stay with me for many days. You shall not play the harlot, nor shall you have a man; so, I will also be toward you."
Hosea 3:1-3 (NAS95)

HERE IS A FAMOUS prophet of The Old Testament, Hosea, being told by God to do something very hard to do at any time. He was told to go marry a woman who is a harlot but also have children who are not his. Now, I'm sure as a man, we've been asked to do many things. But this takes the cake! God wanted Hosea to do this as an example of what the nation of Israel was doing to their God. They left their first love and went whoring after other gods.

Maybe you find yourself in a similar situation with an unfaithful spouse. You've tried to work things out, and it seems to be getting worse, not better. You may feel like throwing in the towel. It may seem hopeless, and you feel helpless. However, I want to encourage you not to give up on God or your spouse. Hosea gives us men a great example of truly how to love someone who is unlovable. Interested in how to take a *trash* situation and allow God to turn it into *treasure* for your marriage?

First, I want to remind you God is still in control. Nothing catches Him by surprise. Just like He knew what would happen to Hosea, He knows what trash is going on in your marriage. He is about to turn it into treasure! Trust God in all things concerning your marriage. God says to us "Be strong and courageous... for the Lord your God is with you wherever you go" (Joshua 1:9). In Hebrew the word *chazq*, means to behave with courage and urgency. Whatever situation you are in won't get fixed by chance; it can only be transformed by choice, by taking heart and stepping forward with courage—no matter what you may be facing.

Second, I want to remind you to be for your wife what God is to us—*faithful*. Just as God is faithful and trustworthy to us, we should be the same way. We need to be *faithful in our love, trustworthy in our walk with our wife,* and *consistent in our marriage*. Stop looking for excuses and start doing what God told you to do and trust Him to work on your wife. Do your part and let God do the rest.

Third, I want to remind you to be like Hosea. We need to have *unfailing love* for our wife. It wasn't about what she did or didn't do, but what He was committed to doing for his wife. Hosea wanted to keep his vow to God and his wife by loving her *unconditionally*. This type of love is based on action. It's faithful. It's reliable. It's loyal. It's consistent. It didn't wait for things to get better. It makes things better! When you pray and do what God says to do for your marriage, it will work out.

Finally, remember your marriage is in God's hands. He will bless it according to what you do as the husband. You're the head of the home. If you are doing as God says, He will cause it to come to pass for your good and his glory. Your marriage will move from trash to treasure. Just as Hosea's wife was in a trash situation, God used her husband to turn her into treasure! So, don't give up on God, because He won't give up on you—nor your marriage. Pray, trust with unfailing, faithful love, and be consistent in obeying what God says. He will turn your marriage into treasure by His grace.

~THINK ABOUT IT~

What are you facing in your marriage today that may look like trash, but God wants to make into *treasure?* You must make a decision to do things for your marriage God's way. God is faithful and trustworthy to fix your marriage. He asks you to do your part and you will see treasure in the form of the marriage you've dreamed about.

Action to Keep Attraction

What actions will you take to incorporate into your marriage the principles, practices, and lessons learned in this chapter? Write out on the lines below things that may be making your marriage trash at this time, and then write down what God says for you to do that can turn them into treasure.

_____

_____

_____

_____

_____

_____

_____

_____

_____

_____

_____

_____

A Prayer for Your Marriage

Father God, help your children seek your will in their marriage and your way for their life. Bless them to know you are the one who turns trash into treasure—no matter how impossible it seems.

Lord, show them your grace, mercy, and love has been a constant and faithful companion in the past, and it will be a bright promise for their future. Help this couple to trust you to make them one and use them for your glory and honor.

It's in Jesus' Name I pray—Amen.

Have You Invested in the Health of Your Marriage TODAY?

Prayer for HIS/HER Heart

A Personal Prayer for Your Spouse and Marriage

Meditate on Song of Solomon 1:15-16. Write out on the lines below your personal prayer for your marriage. Ask God to turn your marriage from trash to treasure for His glory!

Heavenly Father,

_____

_____

_____

_____

_____

_____

_____

_____

_____

_____

_____

_____

_____

_____

Day Twenty

Don't Give Up Now—It's Your Time to Shine!

*And when he had thus spoken, he cried with a loud voice,
"Lazarus, come forth."*

John 11:43

IN THE BEGINNING, WHEN couples share their marriage vows, it's easy to say *"I do"* to a gamut of future commitments with excitement, zeal, and anticipation of a lifetime love affair. But after the passage of several years, that more than likely included many marital ups and downs, some couples might find themselves in a stale marriage where they have grown apart, and the flame of passion has flickered and gone out. Now their starry-eyed promise of *"until death do us part"* seems more like a death sentence rather than a vow of *"forever, I do love you."*

If this seems like the story of your marriage, don't give up now—it's your time to shine! Remember, your story is still being written, so don't put a period where God has only placed a comma. God created marriage to represent Christ's unconditional love for the Church. However, marriage is a process—a process where God uses many things, including your spouse, to build in you a Christlike character. God uses your marital relationship to form you into the image of Jesus—instilling his values, attitudes, and morals within you both. *You can begin again!*

Don't believe the devil's lies when he whispers there is no hope for your marriage to survive. God's grace, mercy, and love has been a constant and faithful companion in the past and still holds a bright promise for your marital future. Expose and expel that which inhibits bringing renewed life to your marriage. Expect the unexpected as you trust God once again to do the miraculous. When you surrender your hearts to God, lay your marriage on the altar of sacrifice and watch Elohim show up in a supernatural way in your marriage. *Now is the time to embrace the unimaginable!*

When you submit your heart and your marriage to God, you are no longer *"self-serving,"* but rather you are willing to selflessly serve your mate. To keep your marriage *"alive"* and *"fresh"* as it was when you both first said, *"I do,"* you must be deliberate and intentional about your actions to fan the marital flames and reignite the passion that may have slipped through the cracks of life.

When was the last time you and your spouse had a really good laugh together? I mean, the kind of laughter that causes tears to flow down your face and your belly to ache. Laughter is a key element in a healthy marriage, and it is good medicine for many ailments—try it and see. *"A merry heart does good, like medicine, but a broken spirit dries the bones."* (Proverbs 17:22).

Lastly, keep sex sacred in your marriage and don't let your "pet peeves" drive you to resent your spouse. I'm talking about those little things that were once upon a time "cute," but now sets your teeth on edge. It's understandable some things that once stirred the flame might now drench the fire. However, time changes things and people too. Your spouse may have changed some over the years but so have you—so try extending grace in the place of judgement and resentment.

Below is a prayer calling forth renewed *LIFE* into your marriage. Take some time to read over this prayer, meditating over the words, and then personalize it to fit your heart's cry for the *REVIVAL* of your marriage.

"COME FORTH!"

LORD, no matter how dead our marriage situation may look, increase my believing faith in your ability to intervene supernaturally and do the impossible. You, ELOHIM, are able to breathe into our dead marriage new life, restore that which the locusts have eaten, and resurrect any dead things.

Jehovah Tsaba—The Lord our Warrior—rise up and wage war against the enemy on behalf of our marriage and family. This day I come crying out to you in prayer, pleading the blood of Jesus over our marriage that is in jeopardy of destruction by the enemy. For I know there is wonder-working POWER in the BLOOD OF JESUS to RESURRECT DEAD things!

Lord, just as You commanded dead Lazarus to *"COME FORTH"* alive again, You have given Your children that same *RESURRECTION POWER* and *AUTHORITY to CALL FORTH* into their marriages those things that are not as though they were and to call that which seems *DEAD* back to *LIFE* again!

Therefore, I CALL FORTH...

LOVE UNCONDITIONAL... COME FORTH!

FORGIVENESS... COME FORTH!

SELFLESSNESS... COME FORTH!

SELF CONTROL... COME FORTH!

PATIENCE... COME FORTH!

GENTLENESS... COME FORTH!

KINDNESS... COME FORTH!

FAITHFULNESS... COME FORTH!

JOY... COME FORTH!

HAPPINESS... COME FORTH!

PEACE... COME FORTH!

COMPASSION... COME FORTH!

IN THE NAME OF JESUS... I DECREE AND DECLARE BY THE POWER OF THE HOLY GHOST... COME FORTH!

I BELIEVE, TRUST, and WALK in the POWER and AUTHORITY You have given me in the strong and mighty NAME OF JESUS! Hear my humble cry this day, oh LORD... Amen!

Action to Keep Attraction

What actions will you and your spouse take to incorporate into your marriage the principles, practices, and lessons learned in this chapter? Write out your goals, plans, and strategies to achieve them on the lines below.

_____

_____

_____

_____

_____

_____

_____

_____

_____

_____

_____

_____

_____

_____

_____

A Prayer for Your Marriage

Father GOD, I come praying you will breathe LIFE into dead marriages and cause husbands and wives to dedicate their lives to you and bring forth FRUITS of a godly marriage that will function as designed by its creator!

Father, we know the enemy is crafty and subtle, but I pray this couple will be as wise as a serpent, as humble as a lamb, and as fierce as a lion when battling satanic forces that come against their marriage, in any and all forms, to destroy their witness and hinder the work of their ordained marriage. Endow this husband and wife with spiritual wisdom, discernment, and understanding. Blot out transgressions and forgive their sins, and restore that which the enemy has stolen from their marriage.

Jehovah Sabaoth—LORD of Hosts! Mighty Guardian... rise up on behalf of this couple to give them the VICTORY in every spiritual battle that comes against their marriage! For you've given us death and life in the POWER of our TONGUES, so help this husband and wife and any other couples who are hurting, discouraged, broken, frustrated, and about to give up and walk out... TO SPEAK LIFE back into their marriage. It's in Jesus' mighty, matchless, and miraculous name I pray! Amen.

> *"Awake, O north wind, and come, O south wind! Blow upon my garden, let its spices flow. Let my beloved come to his garden and eat its choicest fruits."*
>
> Song of Solomon 4:16 (ESV)

Have You Invested in the Health of Your Marriage TODAY?

Prayer for HIS/HER Heart

A Personal Prayer for Your Spouse and Marriage

Heavenly Father,

_____

_____

_____

_____

_____

_____

_____

_____

_____

_____

_____

_____

_____

_____

_____

_____

_____

_____

Day Twenty-One

Tools to Tighten the Ties

Therefore, a man shall leave his father and mother and be joined to his wife, and they shall become one flesh.

Genesis 2:24

PUTTING IT ALL INTO *Action!*

Remember... the key to having a God-centered marriage is not just friendship—*it's ONENESS!* This oneness does not automatically happen in marriage. It must be cultivated. But what does this *oneness* look like? Let's start with the practical definition of *"cultivate."*

- *To **prepare** and **work on** to **raise** or **grow**.*

- *To **seek to promote** or **improve the growth** of by **labor** and **attention**.*

- *To **develop** or **improve by education** or **training; train; refine**.*

- *To **foster the growth** or **development** of.*

- *To **devote oneself** to something or someone.*

Think about some of the keywords in the definition above—*prepare, work on, raise, grow, promote, improve, labor, attention, develop, educate, train, refine, foster,* and *devote.* Now, think about which of those words speak most to you about the areas of your marriage that need work for you and your spouse to grow closer together in oneness. With those areas of lack or need in mind, let's look at **eight ways to help cultivate oneness in your marriage.**

- **Have realistic expectations of your spouse.** No matter what they might project, always remember that your spouse is *"human"* too. They make mistakes, and they do not always have all the right answers to life's questions and problems, especially those relating to your marriage. *Refine your expectations* and always be ready to *extend to them grace...* just as grace has been extended to you through Jesus Christ.

"Since all have sinned and continually fall short of the glory of God and are being justified [declared free of the guilt of sin, made acceptable to God, and granted eternal life] as a gift by His grace [precious, undeserved], through the redemption [the payment for our sin] which is [provided] in Christ Jesus."
Romans 3:23-24 (AMP)

- **Realize God-made differences between you and your spouse.** Your spouse is your life-partner, not your twin. They are not like you, so *seek* to *promote understanding* and not dish out unrighteous judgement and condemnation.

"Then Adam said, 'this is now bone of my bones, and flesh of my flesh; she shall be called Woman, because she was taken out of Man.'"
Genesis 2:23 (AMP)

- **Don't always think the worst about your spouse**. Although the situation may look a certain inevitable way, looks can be deceiving. Try not to jump to unfounded conclusions by playing and replaying the worse scenarios in your mind. Try to *foster* *positive vibes—No Stinking Thinking!*

"She comforts, encourages, and does him only good and not evil all the days of her life."
Proverbs 31:12 (AMP)

- **Don't compare your spouse to how you "wish" they would be.** Living with expectations of a fairytale marriage is not beneficial or expedient to oneness. And certainly, don't fantasize about being married to someone else! The grass isn't always greener on the other side. Learn to *water* your own grass. *Devote* yourself to your spouse *wholeheartedly* and *embrace* them for how God uniquely made them. Pray for God to help you see them through His eyes.

"We do not have the audacity to put ourselves in the same class or compare ourselves with some who [supply testimonials to] commend themselves. When they measure themselves by themselves and compare themselves with themselves, they lack wisdom and behave like fools."
2 Corinthians 10:12 (AMP)

"Drink water from your own cistern [of a pure marriage relationship], and fresh running water from your own well."
Proverbs 5:15, 19 (AMP)

- **Be kind to your spouse, even when you feel they don't deserve it.** Kindness *promotes peace* in your marriage and helps avoid strife, stress, and animosity. Ask yourself these three questions *before* you speak. 1) *Is it True?* 2) *Is it Kind?* 3) *Is it Necessary?*

"Let all bitterness and wrath and anger and clamor [perpetual animosity, resentment, strife, fault-finding] and slander be put away from you, along with every kind of malice [all spitefulness, verbal abuse, malevolence]. Be kind and helpful to one another, tender-hearted [compassionate, understanding], forgiving one another [readily and freely], just as God in Christ also forgave you."

Ephesians 4:31-32 (AMP)

- **Recognize the "real enemy" in your marriage!** Your spouse is not your enemy—Satan is. The real adversary is the devil who seeks to destroy your marriage because of what it represents. God created marriage as a physical representation of Christ's love for the Church. Satan can't destroy God, nor defile Christ's love, so he goes after the next best thing—*your marriage.* Vow here and now that you will not be deceived by the tricks of the enemy and you will make every effort to exemplify the love of Christ in your marriage. Now declare with a loud voice... *SATAN—YOU LOSE!*

"Be sober [well balanced and self-disciplined], be alert and cautious at all times. That enemy of yours, the devil, prowls around like a roaring lion [fiercely hungry], seeking someone to devour."

I Peter 5:8 (AMP)

"Husbands, love your wives [seek the highest good for her and surround her with a caring, unselfish love], just as Christ also loved the church and gave Himself up for her. So that [in turn] He might present the church to Himself in glorious splendor, without spot or wrinkle or any such thing; but that she would be holy [set apart for God] and blameless. This mystery [of two becoming one] is great; but I am speaking with reference to [the relationship of] Christ and the church."

Ephesians 5:25, 27, 32 (AMP)

- **Love Christ *more* than you love your spouse.** It may sound romantic to tell your spouse you love them more than anything or anyone, but is that biblical? Of course not. The Bible teaches we are to love GOD first and with our entire being—with all of our hearts, all of our minds, all of our souls, and all of our might. In other words, *grow* your relationship with God in intimacy and watch your *marriage grow in intimacy* as well. Remember... what you feed will *GROW*, and anything that doesn't *GROW* is dead!

"You shall love the Lord your God with all your heart and mind and with all your soul and with all your strength [your entire being]."

Deuteronomy 6:5 (AMP)

"And walk continually in love [that is, value one another—practice empathy and compassion, unselfishly seeking the best for others], just as Christ also loved you and gave Himself up for us, an offering and sacrifice to God [slain for you, so that it became] a sweet fragrance."

Ephesians 5:2 (AMP)

- **Be determined that divorce will not be an option in your marriage.** I know what you are thinking. Yes, there are biblical grounds for divorce. Sexual immorality *(Matthew 5:32, 19:9)*, and abandonment by an unbelieving spouse *(1 Corinthians 7:15)* are legal and biblical grounds for getting a divorce. And physical (or mental) abuse is certainly not something anyone should be encouraged or required to endure. However, we must never forget what God said in Malachi 2:16, *"I hate divorce, says the Lord God."* In other words, divorce should be a last recourse after you have tried *confession, forgiveness, reconciliation, restoration,* and *counseling.* Commit to resolve problems quickly and never go to bed angry at your spouse. This doesn't mean you will always agree, but resolve to not allow disagreements to override your love—even for a night. Remember... there are always two sides to every story, and your side is only one half of it. *Be encouraged, uplifted, and inspired to* **CULTIVATE YOUR MARRIAGE DAILY!**

"Be angry [at sin—at immorality, at injustice, at ungodly behavior], yet do not sin; do not let your anger [cause you shame, nor allow it to] last until the sun goes down."

Ephesians 4:26 (AMP)

"And above all things have fervent LOVE for one another, for LOVE will cover a multitude of sins."

I Peter 4:8

Action to Keep Attraction

What actions will you and your spouse take to incorporate into your marriage the principles, practices, and lessons learned in this chapter? Write out your goals, plans, and strategies to achieve them on the lines below.

_____

_____

_____

_____

_____

_____

_____

_____

_____

_____

_____

_____

_____

_____

A Prayer for Your Marriage

Heavenly Father, thank you for your righteous right hand that will hold up, cover, protect, and guide this couple safely into your promises for their marriage. For even in the midnight hour, you can and will turn it all around to work in their favor. Help this couple hold on to your unchanging hand and faint not—because that which was meant to destroy their marriage is NOW working in their favor. Hallelujah!

Thank you, ABBA, for your faithfulness to perfect and fulfill every promise for their lives. Help them look to you and you alone to do those everyday miracles in their marriage. This marriage was created to honor and glorify you. Now, show them YOUR GLORY, Oh LORD!

It's in the mighty and matchless Name of Jesus I pray, AMEN!

Have You Invested in the Health of Your Marriage TODAY?

Prayer for HIS/HER Heart

A Personal Prayer for Your Spouse and Marriage

Heavenly Father,

_____

_____

_____

_____

_____

_____

_____

_____

_____

_____

_____

_____

_____

_____

ABOUT THE AUTHORS

REVEREND JAMES A. FORD, Jr. is an ordained, licensed minister who has been a preacher of the gospel for over 35 years. Rev. Ford has a Bachelor of Arts degree from Dallas Baptist University (DBU) with a concentration in Religious Studies. He also holds a Master of Divinity in Biblical Languages with a concentration in Religious Education from Southwestern Baptist Theological Seminary (SWBTS).

Rev. Ford is a preacher-teacher extraordinaire and specializes in Bible Prophecy, World Religions, and Hard Sayings of the Bible. He is a licensed chaplain and has served at various hospitals and at the Federal Bureau of Prisons (FBOP), where he has ministered to patients, inmates, and their families through prayer and biblical counseling.

Mary A. Ford has a Bachelor of Business Administration degree from the University of Houston with concentrations in Marketing and Management. Mary has excelled in a career in Public Administration and Workforce Development for over 35 years. Mary is a seasoned Prayer

Warrior and Bible teacher who has served faithfully in ministry for most of her adult life in various capacities—such as the Music Ministry, Women's Ministry, Discipleship Ministry, Pastoral Care, Christian Education, and Intercessory Prayer Ministry. Since answering God's call to a life of Intercessory Prayer, Mary has served in various capacities as a prayer leader, such as Vice President of Prayer Warriors, Prayer Coordinator, and Prayer Ministry Director, teaching numerous Scripture-based classes and workshops on prayer and leading others to a more intimate relationship with the Father through prayer ministry. Mary is not only a Prayer Warrior, Prayer Leader, and a Teacher of God's Word, she is also an award-winning author—winner of The People's Choice Christian Literary Award for her prayer devotionals.

Rev. James and Mary Ford have served faithfully in ministry together for many years, and in 2014, God called them to launch a new ministry called *"From Duty to Delight: Are You Enjoying Jesus Yet?"* (Aba: D2D Ministries). D2D Ministries is dedicated to Christian discipleship and equipping and encouraging the believer to live a transformed life in Christ through the power of prayer.

Books By Mary A. Ford for Consideration

DUTY TO DELIGHT MINISTRIES by Mary A. Ford—Visit the website for more details at: **www.duty2delightministries**

You may purchase any of the following devotionals and/or study books through the above website or directly from Amazon.

From Duty To Delight: Are You Enjoying Jesus Yet?

ISBN: 978-1498419529

Hour of Power: Moving Your Prayer Life to the Next Level

ISBN: 978-0998330839

Prayer: The Key to Unlocking Blessings (12-Days of Prayer & Fasting—for individuals or groups. Christian Literary People's Choice Award)

ISBN: 978-0998330884

STRENGTH for The Journey: Power for Living a Victorious Christian Life. (Christian Literary Award)

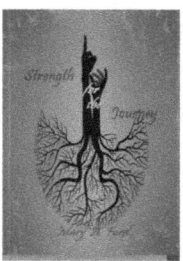

ISBN: 978-1734039825

Thank you to all who have shown love, support, and encouragement along the way. Much Love & Prayers always!

~M. Ford

Most Popular Prayer Classes and Workshops

HOUR OF POWER: TAKING Your Prayer Life to the Next Level

An eight-week Scripture-based prayer curriculum designed to better equip Christians who have a desire to enhance their personal prayer life and pray more effectively. Participants will be challenged to...

- Make prayer a priority in their lives

- Develop consistency in their prayer lives

- Learn to master various prayer elements

- Increase their personal prayer time with God

Prayer That Works

An eight-week Scripture-based prayer curriculum that takes you on a journey through the powerful prayer life of the Old Testament Prophet Elijah. This course is designed to DEVELOP, STRENGTHEN, and ENHANCE the believer's personal relationship with God through the power of prayer. Participants will be challenged to...

- Make prayer a priority through increased personal time with God

- Develop intimacy with God through consistency in prayer

- Strengthen commitment to God through accountability and

prayer partners

- Develop an effective prayer life—praying effectual, fervent Prayers That Work!

Prayer Boot Camp 101

Learn to master the prayer basics through this 90-minute, power-packed prayer workshop. Participants will learn...

- What prayer is

- What prayer does

- What hinders prayer

- What effective prayer requires

- How to get started—developing an effective prayer plan

Praying Together to Stay Together

In this 90-minute marriage workshop, participants will learn the power of prayer in marriage and—True ONENESS! Participants will learn...

- How prayer deepens our relationship with God and one another

- How prayer naturally brings couples into agreement with one another

- How to go before the Lord with our concerns in unity of heart, mind, and spirit!

Prayer: A Prelude to Worship

This 90-minute workshop is designed to take your music ministry and praise team to the next level through the power of prayer and worship! Workshop goals and objectives:

- Reveal the powerful connection that Christians have with God through Prayer

- Explore the significance of prayer in worship

- See how prayer impacts personal and corporate praise and worship

www.ingramcontent.com/pod-product-compliance
Lightning Source LLC
Chambersburg PA
CBHW051202120626
46547CB00012B/1173